On Core
Mathematics

Grade 3

HOUGHTON MIFFLIN HARCOURT

Table of Contents

Operations and Algebraic Thinking

▶ **Represent and solve problems involving multiplication and division.**

▶ **Understand properties of multiplication and the relationship between multiplication and division.**

▶ **Multiply and divide within 100.**

▶ **Solve problems involving the four operations, and identify and explain patterns in arithmetic.**

Number and Operations in Base Ten

▶ **Use place value understanding and properties of operations to perform multi-digit arithmetic.**

Number and Operations - Fractions

▶ **Develop understanding of fractions as numbers.**

Measurement and Data

▶ Solve problems involving measurement and estimation of intervals of time, liquid volumes, and masses of objects.

▶ Represent and interpret data.

▶ Geometric measurement: understand concepts of area and relate area to multiplication and to addition.

► Geometric measurement: recognize perimeter as an attribute of plane figures and distinguish between linear and area measures.

Geometry

► Reason with shapes and their attributes.

1. There are 5 tables in the library. Four students are sitting at each table.

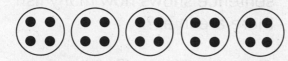

How many students are sitting in the library?

Ⓐ 9   Ⓒ 20

Ⓑ 16   Ⓓ 24

2. Alondra made 3 bracelets. There are 7 beads on each bracelet.

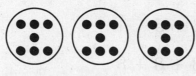

How many beads did Alondra use to make the bracelets?

Ⓐ 10   Ⓒ 21

Ⓑ 14   Ⓓ 24

3. Stella decorated using 4 groups of balloons. She drew this model to show the number of balloons.

How many balloons did Stella use to decorate?

Ⓐ 3   Ⓒ 9

Ⓑ 6   Ⓓ 12

4. Mrs. Bennett sorted spools of thread into 3 containers. Each container held 3 spools.

How many spools of thread does Mrs. Bennett have in all?

Ⓐ 6   Ⓒ 10

Ⓑ 9   Ⓓ 12

5. Cory, Greg, and Carrie each have 4 stickers. Carrie says that she can find how many stickers they have in all by drawing 3 equal groups. How can she use the equal groups to find the number of stickers in all?

_____

_____

_____

Operations and Algebraic Thinking

1. Eric was doing his math homework. Eric wrote:

   $$2 + 2 + 2 + 2 + 2$$

   Which is another way to show what Eric wrote?

   (A) 2×2 (C) 10×2

   (B) 5×2 (D) $5 + 2$

2. Dallas and Mark each sharpened 4 pencils before school.

   Which sentence shows the number of pencils sharpened in all?

   (A) $2 + 2 = 4$ (C) $4 \times 4 = 16$

   (B) $4 + 2 = 6$ (D) $2 \times 4 = 8$

3. A pet store has some fish bowls on display. There are 3 fish in each of 5 bowls. Which number sentence shows how many fish there are in all?

   (A) $5 \times 3 = 15$ (C) $5 + 3 = 8$

   (B) $5 \times 5 = 25$ (D) $3 \times 3 = 9$

4. Carlos spent 5 minutes working on each of 8 math problems. He can use 8×5 to find the total number of minutes he spent on the problems. Which is equal to 8×5?

   (A) $8 + 5$

   (B) $8 + 8 + 8$

   (C) $5 + 5 + 5 + 5 + 5$

   (D) $5 + 5 + 5 + 5 + 5 + 5 + 5 + 5$

5. Ryan bought 4 packages of 3 juice boxes each. Write a multiplication and an addition sentence to show how many juice boxes Ryan bought in all. Explain how your number sentences represent the problem.

   _____

   _____

   _____

   _____

   _____

   _____

Operations and Algebraic Thinking

1. Derek has 12 sweaters. He places an equal number of sweaters into 2 drawers.

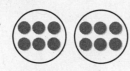

   How many sweaters are in each drawer?

   Ⓐ 2   Ⓒ 6

   Ⓑ 4   Ⓓ 8

2. Megan found 36 seashells. She put an equal number of shells in each of 4 piles. How many seashells are in each pile?

   Ⓐ 32

   Ⓑ 9

   Ⓒ 6

   Ⓓ 4

3. Mr. Jackson has 16 flashcards. He gives an equal number of flashcards to 4 groups.

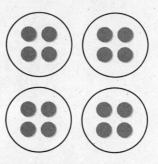

   How many flashcards does Mr. Jackson give to each group?

   Ⓐ 4   Ⓒ 12

   Ⓑ 8   Ⓓ 16

4. Linda picked 48 flowers. She placed them equally into 8 vases. How many flowers are in each vase?

   Ⓐ 4   Ⓒ 6

   Ⓑ 5   Ⓓ 7

5. Nora says you cannot share 9 things in equal groups because 9 is an odd number. Do you agree or disagree? Explain.

   _____

   _____

   _____

   _____

Operations and Algebraic Thinking

1. Elle puts 24 charms into groups of 4. How many groups of charms are there?

   Ⓐ 4

   Ⓑ 6

   Ⓒ 20

   Ⓓ 28

2. A sporting goods store has 72 baseball caps in stacks of 8 caps each. How many stacks of baseball caps are there?

   Ⓐ 7

   Ⓑ 8

   Ⓒ 9

   Ⓓ 11

3. Heather places 32 stamps into groups of 8. How many groups of stamps are there?

   Ⓐ 12

   Ⓑ 8

   Ⓒ 6

   Ⓓ 4

4. Mr. Smith wants to divide his students into groups of 6 for the planetarium tour. How many groups of 6 can be made with 18 students?

   Ⓐ 2

   Ⓑ 3

   Ⓒ 6

   Ⓓ 9

5. Gary says that if you start with an even number of things to divide, you must have an even number of groups. Use an example to show that Gary's idea is wrong.

   _____

   _____

   _____

   _____

1. The Bike Shack displays 45 bikes grouped by color. There are 5 bikes in each group. How many colors of bikes are on display?

_____ colors

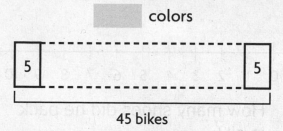

45 bikes

(A) 5   (C) 8

(B) 7   (D) 9

2. Rico went for a 12 mile bike ride. He stopped every 3 miles to take pictures. How many times did Rico stop during his bike ride?

_____ times

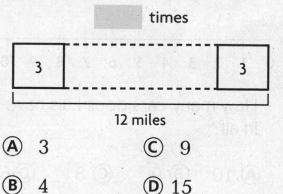

12 miles

(A) 3   (C) 9

(B) 4   (D) 15

3. Amber divided her marbles evenly among 3 friends.

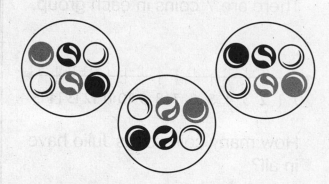

Which division equation is represented by the picture?

(A) $3 \div 3 = 1$

(B) $18 \div 3 = 6$

(C) $18 \div 2 = 9$

(D) $21 \div 3 = 7$

4. There are 16 students in the violin class. Mrs. Lau divides them into 4 equal groups. Explain how the model helps you find how many students are in each group. Write the division equation.

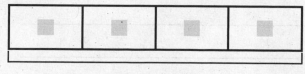

16 students

_____

_____

Operations and Algebraic Thinking

1. Julio has a collection of coins. He puts the coins in 2 equal groups. There are 7 coins in each group.

How many coins does Julio have in all?

Ⓐ 7   Ⓑ 9   Ⓒ 14   Ⓓ 15

2. Mrs. Riley buys 3 packages of mangos to make a large fruit salad. Each package contains 2 mangos.

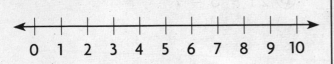

How many mangos does Mrs. Riley have in all?

Ⓐ 4   Ⓑ 5   Ⓒ 6   Ⓓ 8

3. Mr. Walters was cleaning his closet. He packed 2 shoes in each of 5 shoeboxes to donate to charity.

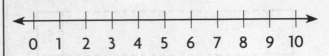

How many shoes did he pack in all?

Ⓐ 3   Ⓑ 7   Ⓒ 9   Ⓓ 10

4. Luis has 3 boxes of cars. There are 3 cars in each box.

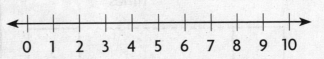

How many cars does Luis have in all?

Ⓐ 10   Ⓑ 9   Ⓒ 8   Ⓓ 6

5. Rochelle makes 5 costumes using 3 yards of fabric for each. Describe how you would use a number line to find the total number of yards of fabric.

_____

_____

_____

1. Carson drew this array to show the number of pictures on one page of her photo album.

Which multiplication sentence does this array show?

Ⓐ $2 \times 3 = 6$ Ⓒ $3 \times 3 = 9$

Ⓑ $4 \times 4 = 16$ Ⓓ $3 \times 2 = 6$

2. Paco drew an array with 3 rows. Each row has 7 squares. Which multiplication sentence describes the array?

Ⓐ $2 \times 8 = 16$ Ⓒ $3 \times 7 = 21$

Ⓑ $2 \times 9 = 18$ Ⓓ $3 \times 8 = 24$

3. Rita arranged counters in 5 rows with 7 counters in each row. Which array shows how many counters she arranged in all?

Ⓐ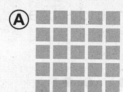

Ⓑ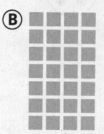

Ⓒ

Ⓓ

4. Geoff stacked 16 cans of paint in 2 rows in his store. He put the same number of cans in each row. Draw an array to show his display.

How many cans of paint are in each row of the display?

Operations and Algebraic Thinking

1. There are 4 tables in the school library. Four students are sitting at each table. Brett made this model with counters to show the total number of students sitting in the library. How many students are sitting in the library?

Ⓐ 8

Ⓑ 10

Ⓒ 12

Ⓓ 16

2. Lily goes on 6 rides at the carnival. The cost of each ride is $2. How much do the rides cost in all?

Ⓐ $14   Ⓒ $10

Ⓑ $12   Ⓓ $8

3. Tara rode her bike to work 4 days this week. She rode a total of 9 miles each day. How many total miles did Tara ride her bike?

Ⓐ 13 miles   Ⓒ 36 miles

Ⓑ 18 miles   Ⓓ 45 miles

4. Max has 4 boxes of pencils. There are 6 pencils in each box. Max draws the model at right to show how many pencils he has in all. Write a multiplication sentence that the model can represent and tell how many pencils Max has in all. Explain how the model represents the sentence you wrote.

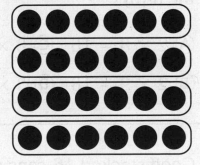

_____

_____

_____

_____

_____

_____

Operations and Algebraic Thinking

1. Kyle bought 4 erasers at the school store. Each eraser cost 10¢.

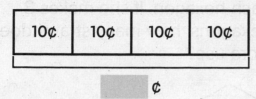

____ ¢

How much did the erasers cost in all?

Ⓐ 14¢   Ⓒ 40¢

Ⓑ 20¢   Ⓓ 44¢

2. Mrs. Howard's students stack their chairs at the end of the day. Each stack contains 5 chairs. If there are 6 stacks of chairs, how many chairs are stacked?

Ⓐ 15   Ⓒ 25

Ⓑ 20   Ⓓ 30

3. Aleesha has 10 packages of beads. There are 6 beads in each package. How many beads does Aleesha have altogether?

Ⓐ 16   Ⓒ 60

Ⓑ 30   Ⓓ 66

4. Tran buys an apple. He gives the store clerk 9 nickels. Each nickel has a value of 5 cents. How many cents does Tran give the store clerk?

Ⓐ 45 cents

Ⓑ 35 cents

Ⓒ 14 cents

Ⓓ 10 cents

5. A gardener draws this picture to show how rose bushes will be planted in three flowerbeds. Each black dot represents one rose bush. How many rose bushes will there be in all? Explain how you used multiplication to find the total number of rose bushes.

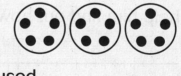

_____

_____

_____

_____

1. Jason has 6 bookshelves in his room. There are 6 books on each shelf. How many books are there in all?

   Ⓐ 12   Ⓒ 36

   Ⓑ 24   Ⓓ 42

2. Madison makes 4 types of hair ribbons. She makes each type of ribbon using 3 different colors. How many hair ribbons does Madison make?

   Ⓐ 12

   Ⓑ 10

   Ⓒ 9

   Ⓓ 7

3. Dora is making hexagons with straws. She uses 6 straws for each hexagon. If she makes 3 hexagons, how many straws does Dora use?

   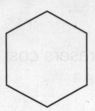

   Ⓐ 9   Ⓒ 18

   Ⓑ 12   Ⓓ 24

4. Elvira bought 4 packages of stickers. There are 6 stickers in each package. How many stickers did Elvira buy?

   Ⓐ 12   Ⓒ 30

   Ⓑ 24   Ⓓ 36

5. Mr. Chung is a florist. He has to make 8 bunches of flowers. He needs 3 feet of ribbon to decorate each bunch. Make a model to help him find out how much ribbon he needs in all.

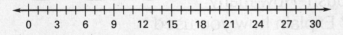

Write a multiplication sentence that the model represents and tell how many feet of ribbon Mr. Chung needs in all. Explain how you used the model to find the answer.

_____

_____

_____

Operations and Algebraic Thinking

1. During a field trip, 30 students in Mrs. Beckman's class were placed into groups of 6 students each for a tour of the museum. How many groups were there?

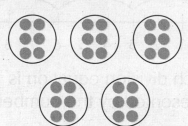

(A) 5   (C) 7

(B) 6   (D) 8

2. Tao has 8 sand dollars in his collection. He makes a model to show how he shares his collection equally with his friend, Yom.

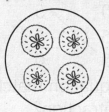 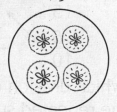

How many sand dollars does each boy get?

(A) 2   (C) 6

(B) 4   (D) 8

3. Barry has 15 comic books. He wants to place his books in 3 equal piles. Which model shows how many comic books Barry should put in each pile?

(A)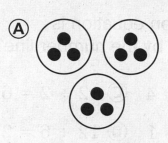

(B)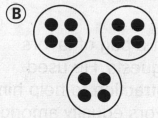

(C)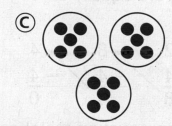

(D)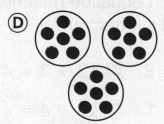

4. There are 54 party favors. Each of 6 tables will have the same number of party favors. How many party favors will go on each table? Explain how you can act out the problem with counters.

_____

_____

Operations and Algebraic Thinking

1. Mr. Burt shared 12 olives equally with each person in his family.

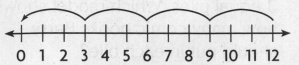

Which division equation is represented by the number line?

Ⓐ 12 ÷ 3 = 4   Ⓒ 12 ÷ 2 = 6

Ⓑ 3 ÷ 3 = 1   Ⓓ 12 ÷ 6 = 2

2. Lionel bought a bag of favors for his party guests. He used repeated subtraction to help him divide the favors equally among his guests.

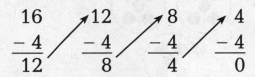

Which division equation matches the repeated subtraction?

Ⓐ 16 ÷ 2 = 8   Ⓒ 12 ÷ 3 = 4

Ⓑ 4 ÷ 4 = 1   Ⓓ 16 ÷ 4 = 4

3. Marco's mother bought 9 toy cars. She asked Marco to share the cars equally among his friends. Marco used a number line to help.

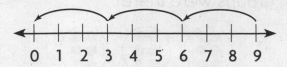

Which division equation is represented by the number line?

Ⓐ 3 ÷ 3 = 1   Ⓒ 9 ÷ 9 = 1

Ⓑ 9 ÷ 3 = 3   Ⓓ 6 ÷ 3 = 2

4. Lola bought a bag of 15 apples for her friends. She used repeated subtraction to help her divide the apples equally among her friends.

$$\begin{array}{ccc} 15 & 10 & 5 \\ -5 & -5 & -5 \\ \hline 10 & 5 & 0 \end{array}$$

Which division equation matches the repeated subtraction?

Ⓐ 15 ÷ 15 = 1   Ⓒ 15 ÷ 5 = 3

Ⓑ 10 ÷ 5 = 2   Ⓓ 15 ÷ 1 = 15

5. How is repeated subtraction like counting back on a number line? Explain how both methods help you divide.

_____

_____

_____

_____

Lesson 13
CC.3.OA.3

1. Which division sentence best fits the array?

Ⓐ $16 \div 16 = 1$

Ⓑ $16 \div 8 = 2$

Ⓒ $16 \div 4 = 4$

Ⓓ $16 \div 1 = 16$

2. Damian has 30 tiles. How many rows of 10 tiles can he make?

Ⓐ 27

Ⓑ 15

Ⓒ 10

Ⓓ 3

3. Which division sentence best fits the array?

Ⓐ $21 \div 1 = 21$

Ⓑ $21 \div 3 = 7$

Ⓒ $20 \div 5 = 4$

Ⓓ $20 \div 10 = 2$

4. The 24 mailboxes in a building are in an array with 6 rows. How many mailboxes are in each row?

Ⓐ 4　　　Ⓒ 8

Ⓑ 6　　　Ⓓ 12

5. Write two division sentences for the array at the right. Explain how the array represents each sentence.

_____

_____

_____

_____

Operations and Algebraic Thinking

1. Lionel has 14 mittens.

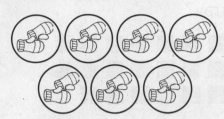

Which division equation is represented by the picture?

Ⓐ 7 ÷ 7 = 1

Ⓑ 2 ÷ 2 = 1

Ⓒ 14 ÷ 14 = 1

Ⓓ 14 ÷ 2 = 7

2. Garret practiced on the piano for the same amount of time each day for 2 days. He practiced a total of 4 hours. How many hours did Garret practice each day?

Ⓐ 1 hour   Ⓒ 6 hours

Ⓑ 2 hours   Ⓓ 8 hours

3. Ben needs 2 oranges to make a glass of orange juice. If oranges come in bags of 10, how many glasses of orange juice can he make using one bag of oranges?

Ⓐ 4   Ⓒ 6

Ⓑ 5   Ⓓ 8

4. Mrs. Conner has 16 shoes.

What division sentence is represented by the picture?

Ⓐ 80 ÷ 8 = 1

Ⓑ 16 ÷ 16 = 1

Ⓒ 16 ÷ 2 = 8

Ⓓ 2 ÷ 2 = 1

5. Hector read for the same amount of time each day for 2 days. He read for 6 hours in all. Explain how to find how many hours Hector read each day.

_____

_____

_____

_____

      Operations and Algebraic Thinking

1. The Bike Shack displays 45 bikes grouped by color. There are 5 bikes in each group. How many colors of bikes does the store have?

   (A) 7

   (B) 9

   (C) 20

   (D) 40

2. Mrs. Alvarez printed 35 pictures. She will group them into sets of 5. How many sets of pictures can she make?

   (A) 40   (C) 7

   (B) 30   (D) 6

3. Hannah made $40 selling hats. Each hat costs $5. She wants to know how many hats she sold. Hannah used a number line to help her.

   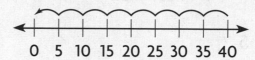

   Which division equation is represented by the number line?

   (A) $6 \div 6 = 1$

   (B) $40 \div 10 = 4$

   (C) $40 \div 4 = 10$

   (D) $40 \div 5 = 8$

4. Tara has 25 fresh muffins. She will freeze them in bags of 5 muffins. Explain how to use the number line to help show how many bags of muffins Tara can freeze.

   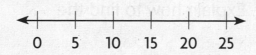

   _____

   _____

   _____

Operations and Algebraic Thinking

1. The volleyball club plans to have 7 teams. There were 42 students who signed up to play. How many students will be on each team?

$$7 \times \blacksquare = 42$$

Ⓐ 5

Ⓑ 6

Ⓒ 7

Ⓓ 8

2. Duane needs 36 hats for a party. There are 6 hats in each package. How many packages of hats does Duane need to buy?

$$p \times 6 = 36$$

Ⓐ 2   Ⓒ 18

Ⓑ 6   Ⓓ 30

3. Pilar spent $48 on 6 books. The cost of each book was the same. Which equation can be used to find the cost of one book?

Ⓐ $48 \times \blacksquare = 6$

Ⓑ $3 \times \blacksquare = 6$

Ⓒ $48 \times \blacksquare = 8$

Ⓓ $6 \times \blacksquare = \$48$

4. Mr. Perkins plans to teach 4 reading groups. If he has 28 students, how many students will be in each reading group?

$$4 \times \blacksquare = 28$$

Ⓐ 24   Ⓒ 7

Ⓑ 8   Ⓓ 6

5. Emily plans to buy 54 muffins for a breakfast party. There are 6 muffins in each package. How many packages will Emily need? Write an equation using the letter p to stand for the unknown factor. Explain how to find the unknown factor.

_____

_____

_____

_____

_____

Operations and Algebraic Thinking

1. Brian is dividing 64 baseball cards equally among 8 friends. How many baseball cards will each friend get?

   Ⓐ 7
   Ⓑ 8
   Ⓒ 9
   Ⓓ 10

2. Adam and his friends raked enough leaves to fill 48 bags. Each person filled 8 bags. How many people raked leaves?

   Ⓐ 6
   Ⓑ 5
   Ⓒ 4
   Ⓓ 3

3. Students celebrated Earth Day by planting 24 seedlings at 8 different locations in town. They planted the same number of seedlings at each location. How many seedlings did they plant at each location?

   Ⓐ 6   Ⓒ 4
   Ⓑ 5   Ⓓ 3

4. Keith arranged 40 toy cars in 8 equal rows. How many toy cars are in each row?

   Ⓐ 4
   Ⓑ 5
   Ⓒ 6
   Ⓓ 32

5. Eight friends planted 72 tulip bulbs. Each friend planted the same number of bulbs. Explain how to find the number of bulbs each friend planted.

   _____

   _____

   _____

   _____

Operations and Algebraic Thinking

1. Donna wrote $5 \times 9 = 45$. Which is a related number sentence?

   Ⓐ $5 + 4 = 9$ Ⓒ $5 \times 5 = 25$

   Ⓑ $9 \times 5 = 45$ Ⓓ $4 \times 5 = 20$

2. Matthew made arrays with counters to show the Commutative Property of Multiplication.

   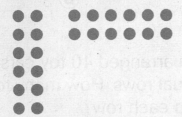

   Which multiplication sentences are shown by his arrays?

   Ⓐ $3 \times 4 = 12$ and $4 \times 3 = 12$

   Ⓑ $6 \times 4 = 24$ and $4 \times 6 = 24$

   Ⓒ $6 \times 2 = 12$ and $2 \times 6 = 12$

   Ⓓ $2 \times 7 = 14$ and $7 \times 2 = 14$

3. Greta put 6 coins into each of 3 stacks. She wrote $3 \times 6 = 18$. Which is a related number sentence?

   Ⓐ $6 \times 3 = 18$

   Ⓑ $6 + 3 = 9$

   Ⓒ $3 + 3 + 3 = 9$

   Ⓓ $6 \times 6 = 36$

4. Ben put 10 color pencils into each of 6 bags. He wrote $6 \times 10 = 60$ to represent the total. Which is a related multiplication sentence?

   Ⓐ $10 \times 10 = 100$

   Ⓑ $5 \times 12 = 60$

   Ⓒ $6 \times 6 = 36$

   Ⓓ $10 \times 6 = 60$

5. Write a multiplication sentence for the array. Then draw a different array you could make using the same two factors. Write the multiplication sentence for the array you drew.

1. Sierra looked in 4 jars for marbles. In each jar she found 0 marbles. Which number sentence represents the total number of marbles Sierra found?

   (A) $4 + 0 = 4$

   (B) $4 \times 0 = 0$

   (C) $4 \times 1 = 4$

   (D) $4 - 4 = 0$

2. Robin found 1 pinecone under each of 3 trees. Which number sentence shows how many pinecones Robin found?

   (A) $3 - 3 = 0$

   (B) $3 + 0 = 3$

   (C) $3 \times 0 = 0$

   (D) $3 \times 1 = 3$

3. Juan bought a golf ball display case with 10 shelves. There are 0 golf balls on each shelf. Which number sentence shows how many golf balls Juan has in the display case now?

   (A) $10 - 0 = 10$

   (B) $1 \times 10 = 10$

   (C) $10 \times 0 = 0$

   (D) $10 + 0 = 10$

4. Aiden saw 4 lifeguard towers at the beach. Each tower had 1 lifeguard. Which number sentence represents the total number of lifeguards Aiden saw?

   (A) $4 \times 4 = 16$

   (B) $4 \times 1 = 4$

   (C) $1 \times 1 = 1$

   (D) $4 + 1 = 5$

5. Franco says that when he multiplies any number by a factor, the product is always equal to the number. What is the factor? Explain how you know this is true.

   _____

   _____

   _____

   _____

Operations and Algebraic Thinking

1. Henry and 5 friends are going to the movies. Tickets cost $8 each. Henry used this model to help him find the total cost of tickets.

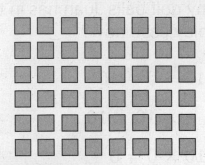

Which shows one way to break apart the array to find the product?

Ⓐ (6 × 5) + (6 × 3)

Ⓑ (3 × 8) + (6 × 8)

Ⓒ (6 × 6) + (6 × 4)

Ⓓ 6 + (4 × 4)

2. Which number sentence is an example of the Distributive Property of Multiplication?

Ⓐ 7 × 8 = 50 + 6

Ⓑ 7 × 8 = 7 × (2 × 4)

Ⓒ 7 × 8 = 8 × 7

Ⓓ 7 × 8 = (7 × 4) + (7 × 4)

3. Which is equal to 7 × 9?

Ⓐ (7 × 3) + (7 × 3)

Ⓑ (7 × 3) × (7 × 3)

Ⓒ (7 × 3) + (7 × 6)

Ⓓ (7 × 3) × (7 × 6)

4. The array at right represents the product 4 × 9. Break apart the array to make two smaller arrays and write a multiplication sentence for each of them. Explain how to use the two smaller arrays to find 4 × 9.

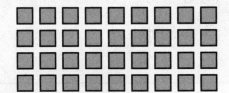

_____

_____

_____

_____

_____

Operations and Algebraic Thinking

1. Which number sentence is an example of the Associative Property of Multiplication?

   (A) $4 \times 2 = 2 \times 4$

   (B) $(4 \times 2) \times 2 = 4 \times (2 \times 2)$

   (C) $4 \times 2 = (4 \times 1) + (4 \times 1)$

   (D) $4 \times (2 + 2) = (4 \times 2) + (4 \times 2)$

2. Which is equal to $(2 \times 2) \times 5$?

   (A) $2 \times (2 + 5)$

   (B) $2 \times (2 \times 5)$

   (C) $(2 \times 2) \times (2 \times 5)$

   (D) $(2 + 5) \times (2 + 5)$

3. Corey has 3 stacks of boxes. In each stack are 3 boxes with 2 trains in each box. How many trains does he have in all?

   (A) 6   (C) 18

   (B) 9   (D) 27

4. There are 2 walls in Yolanda's classroom that each have 2 rows of pictures. Each row has 3 pictures. How many pictures are on these walls in Yolanda's classroom?

   (A) 12   (C) 6

   (B) 7   (D) 4

5. Marshall has 3 bags in each of his 2 toy chests. Each bag has 5 marbles. To find how many marbles there are in all, Marshall writes $(3 \times 2) \times 5$ and $3 \times (2 \times 5)$. Which way can be used to find how many marbles there are in all? Explain your answer.

   _____

   _____

   _____

   _____

   _____

Operations and Algebraic Thinking

1. There are 0 books and 4 bookshelves. How many books are on each bookshelf?

Ⓐ 0   Ⓒ 3

Ⓑ 1   Ⓓ 4

2. Percy paid $9 for some notebooks for school. Each notebook cost $1. How many notebooks did Percy buy?

Ⓐ 0

Ⓑ 1

Ⓒ 8

Ⓓ 9

3. Otis paid $7 for some markers for school. Each marker cost $1. How many markers did Otis buy?

Ⓐ 0

Ⓑ 1

Ⓒ 6

Ⓓ 7

4. Norma made 8 cat treats. She gave an equal number of cat treats to each of 8 cats. How many cat treats did Norma give to each cat?

Ⓐ 0

Ⓑ 1

Ⓒ 4

Ⓓ 8

5. Karen has 5 flower pots and 0 flowers. How many flowers are in each flower pot? Explain. Then write the division sentence.

_____

_____

_____

_____

Operations and Algebraic Thinking

1. Cindy made 24 bracelets using 8 different colors. She made the same number of bracelets of each color. How many bracelets of each color did she make?

   $8 \times \blacksquare = 24$ $24 \div 8 = \blacksquare$

   (A) 2   (C) 4

   (B) 3   (D) 8

2. There are 32 chairs in Mr. Owen's art room. There are 4 chairs at each table. Which equation can be used to find the number of tables in the art room?

   (A) $4 + \blacksquare = 32$

   (B) $32 + 4 = \blacksquare$

   (C) $4 \times 32 = \blacksquare$

   (D) $\blacksquare \times 4 = 32$

3. Yolanda knitted 15 scarves in 3 different colors. She knitted the same number of scarves of each color. How many scarves of each color did she make?

   $3 \times \blacksquare = 15$ $15 \div 3 = \blacksquare$

   (A) 5   (C) 9

   (B) 8   (D) 12

4. Mike wrote these related equations. Which number completes both equations?

   $6 \times \blacksquare = 48$ $48 \div 6 = \blacksquare$

   (A) 9   (C) 7

   (B) 8   (D) 6

5. Write a multiplication equation and a division equation for the array. Explain why those two operations make sense when describing the same array.

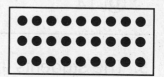

_____

_____

_____

_____

_____

Operations and Algebraic Thinking

1. There are 7 apartments on every floor of Sean's apartment building. The building has 5 floors. How many apartments are in Sean's apartment building?

Ⓐ 12

Ⓑ 21

Ⓒ 35

Ⓓ 42

2. Sandy made greeting cards for a craft show. She put 7 greeting cards in each of 7 boxes. How many greeting cards did Sandy make altogether?

Ⓐ 56

Ⓑ 49

Ⓒ 28

Ⓓ 14

3. Mike sent 7 postcards to each of 4 friends when he was on vacation. How many postcards did Mike send altogether?

Ⓐ 11

Ⓑ 14

Ⓒ 21

Ⓓ 28

4. There are 9 vans taking students to the museum. Each van is carrying 7 students. How many students are in the vans?

Ⓐ 16

Ⓑ 63

Ⓒ 70

Ⓓ 77

5. The students in Ms. Guzman's class picked 6 baskets of peaches. They put 7 peaches in each basket. Write a multiplication sentence to show how many peaches the students picked in all. Explain why a multiplication sentence can be used to represent the total.

_____

_____

_____

Operations and Algebraic Thinking

1. Ashley buys 8 fishbowls. There are 2 goldfish in each bowl. How many goldfish did Ashley buy?

   (A) 4

   (B) 8

   (C) 16

   (D) 24

2. There are 8 teams setting up booths for the school fair. There are 7 people on each team. How many people are setting up booths?

   (A) 28   (C) 56

   (B) 48   (D) 64

3. Students' exhibits at a science fair are judged in 5 categories. Akio's exhibit received 8 points in each category. How many total points did Akio's exhibit receive?

   (A) 20

   (B) 40

   (C) 48

   (D) 56

4. Liz buys 6 flowerpots. There are 8 flowers in each pot. How many flowers did Liz buy?

   (A) 4   (C) 40

   (B) 14   (D) 48

5. There are 8 groups of dogs in a dog show. There are 8 dogs in each group. Jake draws the model at right to show all the dogs in the show. Explain how Jake can use the model and multiplication to find how many dogs there are in all without counting every square in the model.

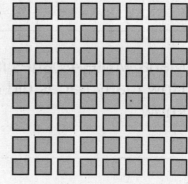

_____

_____

_____

_____

Operations and Algebraic Thinking

1. Mika bought 3 boxes of bouncy balls. Each box contains 9 bouncy balls. How many bouncy balls did Mika buy in all?

   (A) 12

   (B) 18

   (C) 24

   (D) 27

2. There are 8 students in the camera club. Each student took 9 pictures. How many pictures did the students take altogether?

   (A) 81

   (B) 72

   (C) 64

   (D) 17

3. Shana bought 5 bags of hard pretzels. Each bag contains 9 pretzels. How many hard pretzels did Shana buy in all?

   (A) 14

   (B) 40

   (C) 45

   (D) 50

4. Raul has 6 shoeboxes on his bookshelf. If he has 9 toy robots in each shoebox, how many toy robots does Raul have?

   (A) 63

   (B) 54

   (C) 36

   (D) 15

5. Maria wrote 4 pages in her journal each day for 9 days. How many pages did Maria write in all? Explain how you know.

   _____

   _____

   _____

   _____

1. Han wrote a set of related facts for the array below. Which equation is **not** related to this array?

Ⓐ $3 \times 4 = 12$

Ⓑ $6 \times 2 = 12$

Ⓒ $12 \div 4 = 3$

Ⓓ $12 \div 3 = 4$

2. Lucy writes a set of related facts. One of the facts she writes is $24 \div 6 = 4$. Which equation is related to this fact?

Ⓐ $8 \times 3 = 24$

Ⓑ $24 \div 8 = 3$

Ⓒ $6 \times 4 = 24$

Ⓓ $24 \div 3 = 8$

3. Fritz wrote a set of related facts for the array below. Which equation is **not** related to this array?

Ⓐ $6 \times 3 = 18$

Ⓑ $6 \div 2 = 3$

Ⓒ $3 \times 2 = 6$

Ⓓ $2 \times 3 = 6$

4. Alex uses the numbers 3, 4, and 12 to write multiplication and division related facts. Which equation is one of the related facts that Alex writes?

Ⓐ $3 + 4 = 7$

Ⓑ $12 - 8 = 4$

Ⓒ $12 \div 6 = 2$

Ⓓ $4 \times 3 = 12$

5. Peter writes a set of related facts. One of the facts he writes is $18 \div 6 = 3$. Write a division equation that is related to that fact. Explain how an array helps you.

_____

_____

_____

_____

Operations and Algebraic Thinking

1. Larah found 50 pinecones. She put 10 pinecones in each bag. How many bags did Larah use?

   (A) 5

   (B) 6

   (C) 9

   (D) 10

2. Michael wants to display his model car collection on shelves. He has 60 model cars. He puts 10 cars on each shelf. How many shelves does Michael use?

   (A) 6

   (B) 8

   (C) 10

   (D) 70

3. There are 20 students in science class. There are 10 students sitting at each table. Which division sentence shows how many tables have students at them?

   (A) $20 \div 4 = 5$

   (B) $20 \div 10 = 2$

   (C) $10 \div 5 = 2$

   (D) $10 \div 10 = 1$

4. Stickers cost 10¢ each. How many stickers can Todd buy with 80¢?

   (A) 10

   (B) 9

   (C) 8

   (D) 7

5. Vonda says, "I like to divide by 10. The quotient is right there!" Tell what Vonda means by explaining how to solve $90 \div 10$.

   _____

   _____

   _____

   _____

Operations and Algebraic Thinking

1. Steve and his family traveled 12 miles on a sunset cruise. Every 3 miles, the boat stopped for people to take pictures. How many times did the boat stop for pictures?

   Ⓐ 4
   Ⓑ 6
   Ⓒ 9
   Ⓓ 15

2. Martina plays tennis. She gets 21 new tennis balls. They come in cans of 3. How many cans of tennis balls did Martina get?

   Ⓐ 18
   Ⓑ 8
   Ⓒ 7
   Ⓓ 6

3. Jake walked 15 miles in a walk-a-thon. Every 3 miles, he stopped for a rest. How many times did Jake stop for a rest?

   Ⓐ 4
   Ⓑ 5
   Ⓒ 6
   Ⓓ 12

4. There are 27 students in Mr. Garcia's class. The class is going on a field trip to a water park. Mr. Garcia separates the students into groups of 3. How many groups will Mr. Garcia make?

   Ⓐ 30
   Ⓑ 24
   Ⓒ 14
   Ⓓ 9

5. Zelda is teaching her sister about division. Explain how Zelda can use a picture to show how to divide 18 cubes into 3 equal groups.

   _____

   _____

   _____

Operations and Algebraic Thinking

1. Ellen is making 4 gift baskets for her friends. She has 16 prizes she wants to divide equally among the baskets. How many prizes should she put in each basket?

   Ⓐ 4

   Ⓑ 8

   Ⓒ 12

   Ⓓ 20

2. Casey has 20 coins. She places them in equal stacks. There are 4 coins in each stack. How many stacks of coins are there?

   Ⓐ 5

   Ⓑ 6

   Ⓒ 7

   Ⓓ 8

3. Jim collected 28 seashells at the beach. He arranged them in equal rows. There are 4 seashells in each row. How many rows of seashells are there?

   Ⓐ 6

   Ⓑ 7

   Ⓒ 24

   Ⓓ 30

4. Holly is making 4 veggie trays for a party. She wants to divide 36 carrot sticks equally among the trays. How many carrot sticks will she put on each tray?

   Ⓐ 7

   Ⓑ 8

   Ⓒ 9

   Ⓓ 32

5. Mrs. Sosa bought a stuffed toy for each of her 4 grandchildren. She spent $24. Each toy cost the same amount. Explain how to find the cost of each stuffed toy.

   _____

   _____

   _____

1. Pedro uses 30 game pieces to play a game. He gives 6 players the same number of game pieces. How many game pieces does each player get?

   (A) 4   (C) 10

   (B) 5   (D) 15

2. Each team at a hockey tournament has 6 players. How many teams are there if 42 players are at the tournament?

   (A) 5

   (B) 6

   (C) 7

   (D) 8

3. There are picnic tables at the park. Each picnic table seats 6 people. How many picnic tables are needed to seat 24 people?

   (A) 3

   (B) 4

   (C) 5

   (D) 6

4. Luis uses 36 marbles to play a game There are 6 players in the game. If each player gets the same number of marbles, how many marbles does each player get?

   (A) 30   (C) 12

   (B) 18   (D) 6

5. The same number goes in the box in both equations. Explain how to find the unknown factor and quotient using what you know about multiplication and division.

   $$6 \times \blacksquare = 54 \qquad\qquad 54 \div 6 = \blacksquare$$

   _____

   _____

   _____

   _____

1. Ming divided 35 marbles among 7 different friends. Each friend received the same number of marbles. How many marbles did Ming give to each friend?

$$35 \div 7 = a$$

$$7 \times a = 35$$

Ⓐ 4   Ⓒ 6

Ⓑ 5   Ⓓ 7

2. Ana used 49 strawberries to make 7 strawberry milkshakes. She used the same number of strawberries in each milkshake. How many strawberries did Ana use in each milkshake?

Ⓐ 4   Ⓒ 6

Ⓑ 5   Ⓓ 7

3. Joni texted her dad every day for 42 days. How many weeks did Joni text her dad? [Hint: 1 week has 7 days.]

Ⓐ 5 weeks   Ⓒ 7 weeks

Ⓑ 6 weeks   Ⓓ 8 weeks

4. Shang divided 28 postcards among 7 different people. Each person received the same number of postcards. How many postcards did Shang give to each person?

$$28 \div 7 = n$$

$$7 \times n = 28$$

Ⓐ 4   Ⓒ 6

Ⓑ 5   Ⓓ 21

5. The calendar shows the dates in May. Explain how to use the calendar to help find 28 divided by 7.

		May 2011				
Sun	Mon	Tue	Wed	Thu	Fri	Sat
1	2	3	4	5	6	7
8	9	10	11	12	13	14
15	16	17	18	19	20	21
22	23	24	25	26	27	28
29	30	31				

_____

_____

_____

_____

_____

© Houghton Mifflin Harcourt Publishing Company

Operations and Algebraic Thinking

1. Mrs. Torres separates 45 students into 9 equal groups for a field trip. How many students are in each group?

   (A) 4   (C) 6

   (B) 5   (D) 7

2. Carla sells homemade pretzels in bags with 9 pretzels in each bag. She sells 54 pretzels in all. How many bags of pretzels does she sell?

   (A) 6   (C) 4

   (B) 5   (D) 3

3. A flower shop sells tulips in bunches of 9. It sells 27 tulips. How many bunches of tulips does the shop sell?

   (A) 2   (C) 4

   (B) 3   (D) 9

4. There are 36 athletes at a baseball workshop. A baseball team has 9 players. How many teams can be formed?

   (A) 7   (C) 5

   (B) 6   (D) 4

5. Andy keeps mixing up 9 × 9 and 9 × 2. This makes it harder to learn 81 ÷ 9 and 18 ÷ 9. Explain how these multiplication and division facts are alike and how they are different.

   _____
   _____
   _____
   _____
   _____
   _____
   _____

1. During the first week of school, 345 students bought their lunch. During the second week of school, 23 fewer students bought their lunch than the week before. How many students bought their lunch in those two weeks?

   (A) 322   (C) 667

   (B) 368   (D) 713

2. On Monday, 117 students signed up to plant trees in the park. On Tuesday, 16 fewer students signed up than on Monday. How many students signed up to plant trees on Monday and Tuesday?

   (A) 218   (C) 118

   (B) 158   (D) 101

3. In one week, 103 students were absent. The next week, 17 fewer students were absent than the week before. How many students were absent in those two weeks?

   (A) 86   (C) 189

   (B) 120   (D) 223

4. For two days, Imani counted taxis that passed her house from 4:30 to 4:45 P.M. She counted 33 taxis on Monday. That was 19 fewer than the number of taxis she counted on Tuesday. How many taxis did Imani count on both days?

   (A) 14   (C) 52

   (B) 33   (D) 85

5. Draw bar models to solve 45 + 92 = ■ and 92 − ■ = 45. Explain how the models are alike and how they are different.

   _____

   _____

   _____

   _____

Operations and Algebraic Thinking

1. Edith sorts buttons into 4 groups. Each group contains 3 buttons. How many buttons does Edith sort?

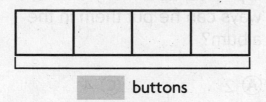

buttons

Ⓐ 4   Ⓒ 12

Ⓑ 11   Ⓓ 16

2. Hector has 4 groups of blocks with 2 blocks in each group. He uses 3 of the blocks for a project. How many blocks does Hector have left?

Ⓐ 3   Ⓒ 9

Ⓑ 5   Ⓓ 11

3. John sold 3 baskets of peaches at the market. Each basket contained 6 peaches. How many peaches did John sell?

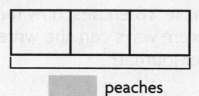

peaches

Ⓐ 36   Ⓒ 18

Ⓑ 30   Ⓓ 9

4. Sophia buys 3 baskets of apples to make applesauce. Each basket has 9 apples in it. How many apples does Sophia buy in all?

Ⓐ 27   Ⓒ 18

Ⓑ 24   Ⓓ 9

5. Landon sorted his trading cards into 3 groups. Each group had 7 cards. How many trading cards does he have in all? Use the bar model to solve. Explain your answer.

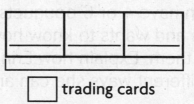

trading cards

_____

_____

Operations and Algebraic Thinking

1. Bella is planning to write in her journal. Some pages will have two journal entries on them, and other pages will have three journal entries on them. If Bella wants to make 18 entries, how many different ways can she write them in her journal?

   (A) 2   (C) 5

   (B) 4   (D) 10

2. Jayme wants to make $1.50 using dollars, half dollars, and quarters. How many different ways can she make $1.50?

   (A) 4   (C) 6

   (B) 5   (D) 7

3. Toddrick has a photo album. Some pages have one photo on them, and other pages have two photos on them. If Toddrick has 9 photos, how many different ways can he put them in the album?

   (A) 2   (C) 4

   (B) 3   (D) 5

4. Myra has 30 cousins. Each month for the past 5 months, she has seen 2 different cousins. How many more cousins does she have to see before she has seen all 30 cousins?

   (A) 18   (C) 25

   (B) 20   (D) 28

5. Erin wants to arrange flower bouquets in rows for a reception. Each row can have 4 or 6 bouquets. She has a total of 22 bouquets and wants to know how many different ways she can arrange them. Explain how Erin could make a table to find how many different ways she can arrange the bouquets.

   _____

   _____

   _____

   _____

   _____

Operations and Algebraic Thinking

1. Gary bought 4 packs of cards. Each pack had the same number of cards. A friend gave him 3 more cards. Now he has 35 cards in all. How many cards were in each pack?

   (A) 42   (C) 8

   (B) 28   (D) 7

2. Mrs. Jackson bought 5 packages of juice boxes. Each package had the same number of juice boxes. She opened one package and gave 3 juice boxes away. Now she has 27 juice boxes. How many juice boxes were in each package?

   (A) 6   (C) 24

   (B) 8   (D) 35

3. Ms. King bought 7 packages of raisin boxes. Each package had the same number of raisin boxes. She opened one package and gave 5 raisin boxes away. Now she has 51 raisin boxes. How many raisin boxes were in each package?

   (A) 56   (C) 8

   (B) 12   (D) 7

4. George had 6 sheets of animal stickers. Each sheet had the same number of stickers. A friend gave him 4 more animal stickers. Now he has 40 animal stickers. How many animal stickers were on each sheet?

   (A) 50   (C) 10

   (B) 24   (D) 6

5. Ruby saved $12 to buy cat toys. Her uncle gives her $3 more. Each cat toy costs $5. Explain the steps needed to find how many cat toys Ruby can buy.

   _____

   _____

   _____

   _____

   _____

Operations and Algebraic Thinking

1. Amber uses the order of operations to solve the equation below.

$$63 - 49 \div 7 = b$$

What is the unknown number?

Ⓐ $b = 2$　　　Ⓒ $b = 55$

Ⓑ $b = 14$　　Ⓓ $b = 56$

2. Aki uses the order of operations to solve the equation below.

$$3 + 12 \div 3 = c$$

What is the unknown number?

Ⓐ $c = 7$　　　Ⓒ $c = 5$

Ⓑ $c = 6$　　　Ⓓ $c = 4$

3. Kayla uses the order of operations to solve the equation below.

$$78 - 54 \div 6 = h$$

What is the unknown number?

Ⓐ $h = 4$　　　Ⓒ $h = 69$

Ⓑ $h = 24$　　Ⓓ $h = 70$

4. Deon uses the order of operations to solve the equation below.

$$3 + 7 \times 3 = x$$

What is the unknown number?

Ⓐ $x = 13$　　Ⓒ $x = 24$

Ⓑ $x = 21$　　Ⓓ $x = 30$

5. Zeke and Luz both found the value of m in this equation:

$$16 - 7 \times 2 = m$$

Zeke says $m = 18$. Luz says $m = 2$. Who is right? Explain your reason.

_____

_____

_____

_____

_____

_____

Operations and Algebraic Thinking

1. Kara wrote this number sentence to show how many yellow stickers and green stickers she earned. Which describes Kara's number sentence?

$$7 + 0 = 7$$

Ⓐ Commutative Property of Addition

Ⓑ Identity Property of Addition

Ⓒ odd + odd = odd

Ⓓ even + even = even

2. Pablo finds the sum of two addends. The sum is odd. Which statement is **true** about the addends?

Ⓐ Both addends are odd.

Ⓑ Both addends are even.

Ⓒ The addends are both odd or both even.

Ⓓ One addend is odd and one addend is even.

3. Maria wrote the number sentence $4 + 7 = 11$. Which number sentence shows the Commutative Property of Addition?

Ⓐ $11 - 4 = 7$

Ⓑ $3 + 4 = 7$

Ⓒ $4 + 7 = 11$

Ⓓ $7 + 4 = 11$

4. Gregory finds the sum of two addends. The sum is even. Which could **not** be Gregory's addends?

Ⓐ $3 + 10$

Ⓑ $7 + 1$

Ⓒ $7 + 7$

Ⓓ $10 + 12$

5. Ruby says she has read an even number of books. She has read 9 fiction books and 8 nonfiction books. Is Ruby correct? Explain your answer.

_____

_____

Operations and Algebraic Thinking

Use the multiplication table for 1–4.

×	0	1	2	3	4	5	6	7	8	9	10
0	0	0	0	0	0	0	0	0	0	0	0
1	0	1	2	3	4	5	6	7	8	9	10
2	0	2	4	6	8	10	12	14	16	18	20
3	0	3	6	9	12	15	18	21	24	27	30
4	0	4	8	12	16	20	24	28	32	36	40
5	0	5	10	15	20	25	30	35	40	45	50
6	0	6	12	18	24	30	36	42	48	54	60
7	0	7	14	21	28	35	42	49	56	63	70
8	0	8	16	24	32	80	48	56	64	72	80
9	0	9	18	27	36	45	54	63	72	81	90
10	0	10	20	30	40	50	60	70	80	90	100

1. Which row of the table has only even numbers?

   Ⓐ the row for 3

   Ⓑ the row for 4

   Ⓒ the row for 7

   Ⓓ the row for 9

2. Which describes a pattern in the column for 5?

   Ⓐ All the products are even.

   Ⓑ All the products are odd.

   Ⓒ Each product is twice the product above it.

   Ⓓ Each product is 5 more than the product above it.

3. Which product is even?

   Ⓐ 3×7

   Ⓑ 4×5

   Ⓒ 5×3

   Ⓓ 9×1

4. Describe as many patterns as you can in the row for 9.

   _____

   _____

   _____

   _____

   _____

1. Lori is making bracelets. The table shows how many beads she will need. Which two numbers come next?

Bracelets	2	3	4	5	6
Beads	10	15	20	■	■

Ⓐ 25 and 30   Ⓒ 30 and 35

Ⓑ 25 and 35   Ⓓ 30 and 40

2. Sofia is making omelets. The table shows how many eggs she will need. Which of the following describes a pattern in this table?

Omelets	2	3	4	5	6
Eggs	6	9	12	15	18

Ⓐ Add 4.   Ⓒ Multiply by 3.

Ⓑ Subtract 3.   Ⓓ Multiply by 4.

3. Stephanie and John made a table about spiders. Which of the following describes a pattern in this table?

Spiders	2	3	4	5	6
Legs	16	24	32	40	48

Ⓐ Add 14.   Ⓒ Multiply by 6.

Ⓑ Subtract 35.   Ⓓ Multiply by 8.

4. Bobby made a table about ants. Which number completes the pattern in this table?

Ants	3	4	5	6	7
Legs	18	24	30	■	42

Ⓐ 6   Ⓒ 36

Ⓑ 35   Ⓓ 40

5. One vase holds 5 roses. Complete the table to find the number of roses in 7 vases. Write the number of roses in 7 vases.

Vases	1	2	3				
Roses	5	10	15				

_____ roses

1. On Friday, 209 people attended a show. What is 209 rounded to the nearest ten?

   (A) 100

   (B) 200

   (C) 210

   (D) 220

2. There are 852 mystery books in the school library. What is 852 rounded to the nearest ten?

   (A) 800

   (B) 850

   (C) 860

   (D) 900

3. There are 487 books in the classroom library. What is 487 rounded to the nearest ten?

   (A) 480

   (B) 490

   (C) 500

   (D) 510

4. Pizza Place sold 581 pizzas on Friday night. What is 581 rounded to the nearest hundred?

   (A) 600

   (B) 590

   (C) 580

   (D) 500

5. Dan has saved $143. If he rounds $143 to the nearest ten, he gets one number. If he rounds it to the nearest hundred, he gets another number. Explain how one amount can be rounded two different ways.

   _____

   _____

   _____

   _____

1. Amber and her friends collected shells. The table shows how many shells each person collected.

Shells Collected

Name	Number of Shells
Amber	372
Melba	455
Pablo	421
Tom	515

Which is the **best** estimate of the total number of shells Amber and Pablo collected?

Ⓐ 600 Ⓒ 800

Ⓑ 700 Ⓓ 900

2. The parking lot at the grocery store had 574 parking spaces. Another 128 parking spaces were added to the parking lot. Which is the **best** estimate of the total number of parking spaces in the parking lot now?

Ⓐ 800 Ⓒ 600

Ⓑ 700 Ⓓ 500

3. Mavis and her friends collected bottle caps. The table shows how many bottle caps each person collected.

Bottle Caps Collected

Name	Number of Bottle Caps
Karen	372
Mavis	255
Pedro	121
John	315

Which is the **best** estimate of the total number of bottle caps Mavis and Pedro collected?

Ⓐ 100 Ⓒ 300

Ⓑ 200 Ⓓ 400

4. Umiko made 47 origami birds last week and 62 origami birds this week. About how many origami birds did she make in the two weeks?

Ⓐ 10 Ⓒ 110

Ⓑ 60 Ⓓ 200

5. Bruce wants to use compatible numbers to estimate 173 + 327. Suggest two compatible numbers he could use to estimate the sum. Explain your choices.

_____

_____

_____

Number and Operations in Base Ten

1. Three classes had a reading contest. The table shows how many books the students in each class read.

Reading Contest

Class	Number of Books
Mr. Lopez	273
Ms. Martin	403
Mrs. Wang	147

Which is the **best** estimate of how many more books Ms. Martin's class read than Mr. Lopez's class?

Ⓐ 100 　　Ⓒ 300

Ⓑ 200 　　Ⓓ 400

2. Abby and Cruz are playing a game. Abby's score is 168 points less than Cruz's score. Cruz's score is 754. Which is the **best** estimate of Abby's score?

Ⓐ 300 　　Ⓒ 500

Ⓑ 400 　　Ⓓ 600

3. Three classes had a spelling contest. The table shows how many words the students in each class spelled correctly.

Spelling Contest

Class	Number of Words
Mr. Silva	719
Ms. Parker	660
Mrs. Cheng	847

Which is the **best** estimate of how many more words Mrs. Cheng's class spelled correctly than Mr. Silva's class?

Ⓐ 100 　　Ⓒ 300

Ⓑ 200 　　Ⓓ 400

4. Andre and Salma collect stamps. Andre has 287 stamps. Salma has 95 stamps. About how many more stamps does Andre have than Salma has?

Ⓐ 400 　　Ⓒ 200

Ⓑ 300 　　Ⓓ 100

5. To estimate 512 − 87, Kim rounded the numbers to 510 − 90 and subtracted. What is another way that Kim could have estimated to subtract? Explain why it might be easier.

_____

_____

_____

Number and Operations in Base Ten

1. On Monday, 114 girls and 205 boys wore jeans to school. How many students wore jeans to school on Monday?

   (A) 219

   (B) 299

   (C) 309

   (D) 319

2. The snack stand has 28 honey granola bars and 42 maple granola bars. How many granola bars does the snack stand have in all?

   (A) 60

   (B) 68

   (C) 70

   (D) 78

3. The Smoothie Stop sold 216 banana smoothies and 132 peach smoothies for breakfast. How many banana smoothies and peach smoothies did the Smoothie Stop sell combined?

   (A) 358

   (B) 348

   (C) 339

   (D) 248

4. There are 37 second graders and 27 third graders in the soccer club. How many students are in the soccer club?

   (A) 54

   (B) 64

   (C) 67

   (D) 74

5. Aya has to find the sum of $67 + 34$. Explain a mental math strategy she can use to find the sum.

   _____

   _____

   _____

   _____

Number and Operations in Base Ten

1. Amy writes a number sentence that shows the Commutative Property of Addition. Which could be Amy's number sentence?

   Ⓐ $(53 + 9) + 41 = 53 + (9 + 41)$

   Ⓑ $53 + 0 = 53$

   Ⓒ $41 = 40 + 1$

   Ⓓ $53 + 9 = 9 + 53$

2. Mr. Rios bought 24 apples, 16 bananas, and 14 pears at the store. How many pieces of fruit did he buy?

   Ⓐ 64

   Ⓑ 54

   Ⓒ 40

   Ⓓ 38

3. Mario writes a number sentence that shows the Commutative Property of Addition. Which could be Mario's number sentence?

   Ⓐ $37 = 36 + 1$

   Ⓑ $0 + 23 = 23$

   Ⓒ $37 + 13 = 13 + 37$

   Ⓓ $(37 + 13) + 23 = 37 + (13 + 23)$

4. John writes the following number sentences. Which shows the Associative Property of Addition?

   Ⓐ $7 + (13 + 8) = (7 + 13) + 8$

   Ⓑ $44 + (56 + 13) = 44 + (13 + 56)$

   Ⓒ $44 + 56 = 40 + 60$

   Ⓓ $44 + 56 = 100$

5. A ferry carries 47 cars, 28 vans, and 13 trucks to an island. Explain the addition property you would use to find the total number of vehicles on the ferry.

_____

_____

_____

_____

Number and Operations in Base Ten

1. A Rent-A-Raft store rented 213 rafts in June and 455 rafts in July. How many rafts did the Rent-A-Raft store rent in June and July altogether?

   (A) 658

   (B) 668

   (C) 678

   (D) 778

2. Omar wants to break apart the addend 362 to complete an addition problem. Which shows a way to break apart the addend 362?

   (A) 3 + 6 + 2

   (B) 300 + 60 + 20

   (C) 30 + 62

   (D) 300 + 60 + 2

3. Marcus took 242 pictures with his new camera and 155 pictures with his camera phone. How many pictures did Marcus take in all?

   (A) 397

   (B) 387

   (C) 297

   (D) 292

4. The number of campers at Arrowhead Camp was 412 in July and 443 in August. How many campers were at Arrowhead Camp in July and August combined?

   (A) 865

   (B) 855

   (C) 843

   (D) 455

5. Explain how you can tell that the sum of 575 and 338 is greater than 900 without finding the exact sum.

   _____

   _____

   _____

   _____

Number and Operations in Base Ten

1. The table shows the number of students visiting the zoo each day.

Field Trips This Week

Day	Number of Students
Monday	346
Tuesday	518
Wednesday	449
Thursday	608

How many students will visit the zoo on Monday and Tuesday combined?

Ⓐ 814   Ⓒ 864

Ⓑ 854   Ⓓ 964

2. Mr. Rodriguez drove 136 miles to Main City. Then he drove another 146 miles to Rock Town. How many miles did Mr. Rodriguez drive?

Ⓐ 212 miles   Ⓒ 272 miles

Ⓑ 270 miles   Ⓓ 282 miles

3. The table shows the number of students who bought lunch in the school cafeteria one week.

Bought Lunch in Cafeteria

Day	Number of Students
Monday	236
Tuesday	319
Wednesday	225
Thursday	284
Friday	306

How many students bought lunch in the cafeteria on Wednesday and Friday combined?

Ⓐ 261   Ⓒ 531

Ⓑ 521   Ⓓ 631

4. Mrs. Carlson drove 283 miles to Plant City. She then drove 128 miles to Bond Town. How far did Mrs. Carlson drive?

Ⓐ 411 miles   Ⓒ 365 miles

Ⓑ 401 miles   Ⓓ 311 miles

5. Bryce has 317 baseball cards. Elin has 168 baseball cards and Jeff has 425 baseball cards. Which two people together have fewer than 500 cards? Explain your answer.

_____

_____

_____

Number and Operations in Base Ten

1. Mikio drove a total of 267 miles in 2 days. He drove 125 miles the first day. How many miles did he drive the second day?

   Ⓐ 142 miles

   Ⓑ 162 miles

   Ⓒ 242 miles

   Ⓓ 392 miles

2. The Fruity Yogurt Company sold 86 banana yogurt bars and 47 strawberry yogurt bars. How many more banana yogurt bars were sold than strawberry yogurt bars?

   Ⓐ 49   Ⓒ 39

   Ⓑ 41   Ⓓ 31

3. The Party Popcorn Company sold 58 bags of cheese popcorn and 39 bags of nutty popcorn. How many more bags of cheese popcorn were sold than nutty popcorn?

   Ⓐ 97

   Ⓑ 41

   Ⓒ 29

   Ⓓ 19

4. Lin drove a total of 346 miles in 2 days. She drove 204 miles the first day. How many miles did she drive the second day?

   Ⓐ 142 miles   Ⓒ 173 miles

   Ⓑ 152 miles   Ⓓ 322 miles

5. Kizzy tried to use friendly numbers to subtract 76 − 28. She added 2 to 28 to change it to 30. So she subtracted 2 from 76. Find the error in Kizzy's strategy. Tell how to use friendly numbers to find this difference.

   _____

   _____

   _____

   _____

   _____

Number and Operations in Base Ten

1. The school store had 136 notepads. It sold 109 notepads. How many notepads are left?

(A) 27

(B) 33

(C) 37

(D) 43

2. Mr. Ruiz's art students used 159 green beads and 370 orange beads to make necklaces. How many more orange beads than green beads did they use?

(A) 201

(B) 211

(C) 221

(D) 229

3. The craft store had 151 bags of beads. It sold 128 bags. How many bags of beads are left?

(A) 37

(B) 33

(C) 27

(D) 23

4. A movie theater has 245 seats in the main section, and 78 seats up in the balcony. How many more seats are in the main section?

(A) 137

(B) 167

(C) 187

(D) 233

5. Should Ally regroup to subtract 647 − 284? Explain how you know without doing the subtraction. Then tell the steps to find the difference.

_____

_____

_____

_____

_____

© Houghton Mifflin Harcourt Publishing Company

1. Students want to sell 420 tickets to the school fair. They have sold 214 tickets. How many more tickets do they need to sell to reach their goal?

   (A) 106

   (B) 206

   (C) 214

   (D) 634

2. A website received 724 visitors last month. This month, there were 953 visitors. How many more visitors did the website have this month than last month?

   (A) 1,677   (C) 229

   (B) 231   (D) 129

3. The owners of a new discount store expect 350 shoppers the day the store opens. By noon, there are 143 shoppers. How many more shoppers do they need to reach their goal?

   (A) 107

   (B) 207

   (C) 217

   (D) 223

4. A popular ride at a theme park has 200 seats. Only 84 people got tickets for the last ride of the day. How many empty seats were there?

   (A) 184   (C) 126

   (B) 124   (D) 116

5. Neo was asked to find 864 − 557. Explain how he can use the *combine place values* strategy to find the difference.

   _____

   _____

   _____

   _____

1. Uncle Tito has 4 nephews. He gives each boy a $30 gift card to a hobby shop. What is the total cost of the 4 gift cards?

   Ⓐ $34   Ⓒ $120

   Ⓑ $80   Ⓓ $150

2. A toy store has 4 shelves of stuffed animals on display. Each shelf displays 20 stuffed animals. Which diagram shows a way to find the total number of stuffed animals on display?

   Ⓐ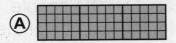

   Ⓑ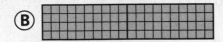

   Ⓒ

   Ⓓ

3. Wendy buys 7 boxes of envelopes. There are 80 envelopes in each box. How many envelopes does Wendy buy altogether?

   Ⓐ 56   Ⓒ 630

   Ⓑ 560   Ⓓ 640

4. Aunt Sonya has 5 nieces. She gives each girl a $40 gift card to the museum shop. What is the total cost of the 5 gift cards?

   Ⓐ $45

   Ⓑ $50

   Ⓒ $160

   Ⓓ $200

5. Corey sold 5 kites to each of 20 people. How many kites did Corey sell altogether? Explain your answer.

   _____

   _____

   _____

   _____

1. Lucia takes care of farm animals. She works 5 days each week. Last week she took care of 60 farm animals each day she worked. How many farm animals did Lucia take care of last week?

   (A) 360   (C) 240

   (B) 300   (D) 65

3. Each school bus has seats for 30 students. On a recent third-grade field trip, 7 buses were filled with students. How many students went on the field trip?

   (A) 21   (C) 180

   (B) 37   (D) 210

2. What multiplication sentence does the model show?

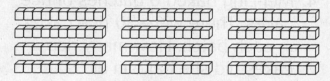

   (A) 3 × 4 = 12

   (B) 2 × 60 = 120

   (C) 3 × 40 = 120

   (D) 4 × 30 = 120

4. What multiplication sentence does the model show?

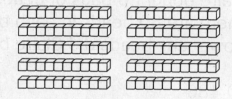

   (A) 2 × 5 = 10

   (B) 3 × 40 = 120

   (C) 2 × 50 = 100

   (D) 2 × 60 = 120

5. Mark drew this number line to find 2 × 60. Explain how Mark can use the number line to find the answer.

```
◄——┼——┼——┼——┼——┼——┼——┼——┼——┼——┼——┼——┼——┼——┼——┼——►
    0   10  20  30  40  50  60  70  80  90  100 110 120 130 140 150
```

_____

_____

_____

_____

Number and Operations in Base Ten

1. A bank makes rolls of 40 nickels. How many nickels would there be in 8 rolls?

(A) 640

(B) 320

(C) 80

(D) 64

2. Claire bought 6 bags of beads. There are 80 beads in each bag. How many beads did Claire buy?

(A) 480

(B) 460

(C) 400

(D) 380

3. Mr. Chandler planted 5 rows of bean seedlings. He planted 50 seedlings in each row. How many seedlings did Mr. Chandler plant?

(A) 55

(B) 200

(C) 250

(D) 350

4. Mei-Ling baked 6 batches of rice cakes. There were 30 rice cakes in each batch. How many rice cakes did she bake in all?

(A) 36

(B) 120

(C) 150

(D) 180

5. One pack of index cards has 80 cards. Explain how to find out how many cards are in 8 packs.

_____

_____

_____

_____

1. This shape is divided into equal parts.

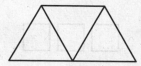

What is the name for the parts?

(A) eighths (C) halves

(B) fourths (D) thirds

2. This shape is divided into equal parts.

What is the number of equal parts?

(A) 8 (C) 3

(B) 4 (D) 2

3. Jamal folded a piece of cloth into equal parts.

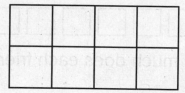

What is the name for the parts?

(A) eighths (C) thirds

(B) fourths (D) halves

4. Kwan folded a circle into equal parts.

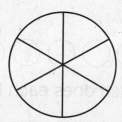

What is the name for the parts?

(A) eighths (C) fourths

(B) sixths (D) thirds

5. Hannah has a square cloth. Describe two ways she could divide it into four equal parts.

_____

_____

_____

1. Three friends share 6 graham crackers equally.

   ☐ ☐ ☐ ☐ ☐ ☐

   How much does each friend get?

   Ⓐ 2 wholes

   Ⓑ 2 wholes and 1 half

   Ⓒ 3 wholes

   Ⓓ 3 wholes and 1 half

2. Four brothers share 5 cookies equally.

   ◯ ◯ ◯ ◯ ◯

   How much does each brother get?

   Ⓐ 1 whole and 1 fifth

   Ⓑ 1 whole and 1 fourth

   Ⓒ 1 whole and 2 fourths

   Ⓓ 1 whole and 4 fifths

3. Four friends share 3 fruit bars equally.

   ☐ ☐ ☐

   How much does each friend get?

   Ⓐ 1 third

   Ⓑ 2 thirds

   Ⓒ 3 fourths

   Ⓓ 5 eighths

4. Three teachers share 7 brownies equally.

   ☐ ☐ ☐ ☐ ☐ ☐ ☐

   How much does each teacher get?

   Ⓐ 1 whole and 1 third

   Ⓑ 1 whole and 2 thirds

   Ⓒ 2 wholes and 1 third

   Ⓓ 2 wholes and 2 thirds

5. Two moms share 3 sandwiches equally.

   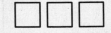

   Shade the squares to show how much each mom gets. Then write the answer.

   _____

© Houghton Mifflin Harcourt Publishing Company

Number and Operations–Fractions

1. The shaded part of the model shows how much cornbread was left after dinner.

   What fraction of the cornbread was left?

   (A) $\frac{1}{3}$ (C) $\frac{1}{6}$

   (B) $\frac{1}{4}$ (D) $\frac{1}{8}$

2. Riley shaded a model to show the amount of sandwich she ate.

   What fraction of the sandwich did Riley eat?

   (A) $\frac{1}{4}$ (C) $\frac{1}{2}$

   (B) $\frac{1}{3}$ (D) $\frac{1}{1}$

3. Kareena made potato salad. She shaded a model to show how much salad was left.

   What fraction of the potato salad was left?

   (A) $\frac{1}{2}$ (C) $\frac{1}{6}$

   (B) $\frac{1}{4}$ (D) $\frac{1}{8}$

4. The shaded part of the model shows how many paintings were sold at an art show.

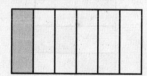

   What fraction of the paintings were sold?

   (A) $\frac{1}{6}$ (C) $\frac{1}{4}$

   (B) $\frac{1}{5}$ (D) $\frac{1}{3}$

5. Mario drew a model to represent $\frac{1}{3}$ of the space in his bookcase. How could Mario draw a model to represent all the space in his bookcase?

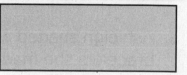

   _____

   _____

   _____

Number and Operations–Fractions

1. What fraction names the shaded part of the page?

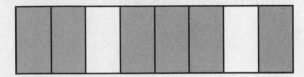

    Ⓐ eight sixths

    Ⓑ eight eighths

    Ⓒ six eighths

    Ⓓ two sixths

2. Lilly shaded this model to show what part of all the books she read are fiction.

What fraction of the books Lilly read are fiction?

    Ⓐ $\frac{3}{3}$ Ⓒ $\frac{3}{4}$

    Ⓑ $\frac{5}{6}$ Ⓓ $\frac{3}{6}$

3. What fraction names the shaded part of the shape?

    Ⓐ three eighths

    Ⓑ five eighths

    Ⓒ six eighths

    Ⓓ eight eighths

4. Bailey shaded this model to show what part of all the baseball games his team won last season.

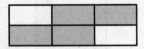

What fraction of the games did Bailey's team win?

    Ⓐ $\frac{2}{6}$ Ⓒ $\frac{4}{6}$

    Ⓑ $\frac{2}{4}$ Ⓓ $\frac{6}{4}$

5. Ashleigh shaded a model to show what part of the bracelets she made are blue. Explain how the model can be used to describe what part of the bracelets Ashleigh made are not blue.

_____

_____

        Number and Operations–Fractions

1. There are 8 rows of chairs in the auditorium. Three of the rows are empty. What fraction of the rows of chairs are empty?

   Ⓐ $\frac{5}{8}$ Ⓒ $\frac{3}{8}$

   Ⓑ $\frac{4}{8}$ Ⓓ $\frac{1}{8}$

2. Greyson has 3 baseballs. He brings 2 baseballs to school. What fraction of his baseballs does Greyson bring to school?

   Ⓐ $\frac{1}{3}$ Ⓒ $\frac{2}{3}$

   Ⓑ $\frac{1}{2}$ Ⓓ $\frac{3}{2}$

3. David sold 6 apple trees. He sold 5 of the apple trees to Max. What fraction of the apple trees did David sell to Max?

   Ⓐ $\frac{1}{6}$ Ⓒ $\frac{5}{6}$

   Ⓑ $\frac{3}{16}$ Ⓓ $\frac{6}{5}$

4. Maria has 8 tulip bulbs. She gives 3 of the tulip bulbs to her neighbor. What fraction of her tulip bulbs does Maria give to her neighbor?

   Ⓐ $\frac{3}{8}$ Ⓒ $\frac{3}{5}$

   Ⓑ $\frac{5}{8}$ Ⓓ $\frac{8}{3}$

5. Diana writes $\frac{1}{4}$ to describe the group of balloons shown below. What could Diana be describing? Explain your reasoning.

   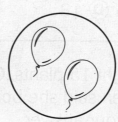

_____

_____

_____

Number and Operations–Fractions

1. Charlotte bought 16 songs. One fourth of the songs are pop songs.

How many of the songs are pop songs?

Ⓐ 16   Ⓒ 4

Ⓑ 12   Ⓓ 1

2. Sophie uses 18 beads to make a necklace. One sixth of the beads are purple. How many of the beads are purple?

Ⓐ 1   Ⓒ 6

Ⓑ 3   Ⓓ 18

3. Mr. Walton ordered 12 pizzas for the art class celebration. One fourth of the pizzas had only mushrooms.

How many of the pizzas had only mushrooms?

Ⓐ 1   Ⓒ 4

Ⓑ 3   Ⓓ 9

4. Caleb took 24 photos at the zoo. One eighth of his photos are of giraffes. How many of Caleb's photos are of giraffes?

Ⓐ 1   Ⓒ 8

Ⓑ 3   Ⓓ 24

5. Mrs. Green bought 15 plants. One third of them were tomato plants. Mrs. Green said she bought 5 tomato plants. Do you agree? Explain your answer.

_____

_____

_____

Number and Operations–Fractions

1. Samuel brought 2 autographed baseballs for show and tell. They are $\frac{1}{6}$ of his whole collection. How many autographed baseballs are in Samuel's whole collection?

   Ⓐ 3   Ⓒ 12

   Ⓑ 4   Ⓓ 13

2. Together, Dillon and Leon make up $\frac{1}{4}$ of the midfielders on the soccer team. How many midfielders are on the team?

   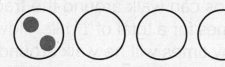

   Ⓐ 2   Ⓒ 6

   Ⓑ 4   Ⓓ 8

3. Ben has 12 model cars in his room. These cars represent $\frac{1}{2}$ of the model cars in Ben's whole collection. How many model cars does Ben have in his whole collection?

   Ⓐ 24   Ⓒ 15

   Ⓑ 18   Ⓓ 6

4. A garden has 2 yellow rose plants. These rose plants represent $\frac{1}{8}$ of the plants in the entire garden. How many plants are in the entire garden?

   Ⓐ 4   Ⓒ 10

   Ⓑ 6   Ⓓ 16

5. Laura found 5 shells on a trip to the beach. These shells represent $\frac{1}{3}$ of the shells in her whole collection. How many shells does Laura have in her whole collection? Draw a diagram to find the answer.

Number and Operations–Fractions

1. Which fraction names point *A* on the number line?

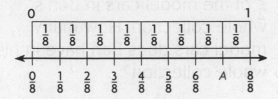

Ⓐ $\frac{1}{8}$ Ⓒ $\frac{7}{8}$

Ⓑ $\frac{6}{8}$ Ⓓ $\frac{8}{8}$

2. Which fraction names point *A* on the number line?

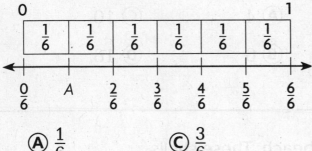

Ⓐ $\frac{1}{6}$ Ⓒ $\frac{3}{6}$

Ⓑ $\frac{2}{6}$ Ⓓ $\frac{1}{1}$

3. Lucy can ride her bike around the block 4 times for a total of 1 mile. How many times will she ride around the block to go $\frac{3}{4}$ mile?

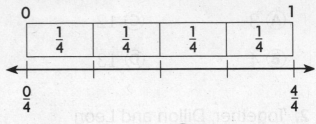

Ⓐ 2   Ⓒ 6

Ⓑ 3   Ⓓ 8

4. Carlos can walk around the track 8 times for a total of 1 mile. How many times will he walk around the track to go $\frac{7}{8}$ mile?

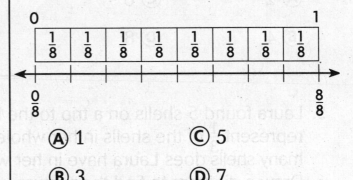

Ⓐ 1   Ⓒ 5

Ⓑ 3   Ⓓ 7

5. Fruit bars come 3 bars to a package. Explain how to use the number line to find how many fruit bars Tara would eat to finish $\frac{2}{3}$ of a package.

0			1
$\frac{1}{3}$	$\frac{1}{3}$	$\frac{1}{3}$	

$\frac{0}{3}$ $\frac{3}{3}$

_____

_____

_____

1. Brenda paints $\frac{1}{2}$ of a wall green.

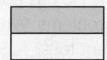

Which fraction is equivalent to $\frac{1}{2}$?

Ⓐ $\frac{4}{8}$ Ⓒ $\frac{2}{1}$

Ⓑ $\frac{1}{6}$ Ⓓ $\frac{2}{6}$

3. Ming-Na has read $\frac{2}{3}$ of a book. Glenn has read the same amount of the book.

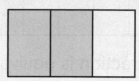

Which fraction is equivalent to $\frac{2}{3}$?

Ⓐ $\frac{1}{2}$ Ⓒ $\frac{3}{4}$

Ⓑ $\frac{5}{8}$ Ⓓ $\frac{4}{6}$

2. Maria has $\frac{1}{2}$ of an obstacle course left to finish.

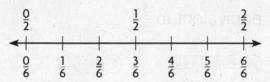

Which fraction is equivalent to $\frac{1}{2}$?

Ⓐ $\frac{2}{1}$ Ⓒ $\frac{3}{6}$

Ⓑ $\frac{2}{6}$ Ⓓ $\frac{5}{6}$

4. Mrs. Reid needs $\frac{3}{4}$ cup of brown sugar for a recipe.

Which fraction is equivalent to $\frac{3}{4}$?

Ⓐ $\frac{7}{8}$ Ⓒ $\frac{3}{8}$

Ⓑ $\frac{6}{8}$ Ⓓ $\frac{4}{3}$

---

5. Use the fraction circles to complete the statement.

$\frac{1}{4} = \frac{\square}{8}$

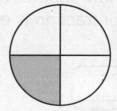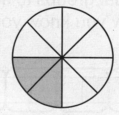

Explain how the numerators and denominators are related in the equivalent fractions.

_____

_____

Number and Operations—Fractions

1. Sam went for a ride on a sailboat. The ride lasted $\frac{3}{4}$ hour.

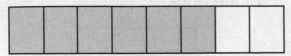

   Which fraction is equivalent to $\frac{3}{4}$?

   Ⓐ $\frac{3}{6}$ Ⓒ $\frac{3}{8}$

   Ⓑ $\frac{4}{8}$ Ⓓ $\frac{6}{8}$

2. Tom rode his horse for $\frac{4}{6}$ mile. Liz rode her horse for an equal distance.

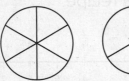

   Which fraction is equivalent to $\frac{4}{6}$?

   Ⓐ $\frac{1}{3}$ Ⓒ $\frac{2}{6}$

   Ⓑ $\frac{2}{3}$ Ⓓ $\frac{4}{3}$

3. Pedro is doing his math homework. He has completed $\frac{8}{8}$ of the problems. Which fraction is equivalent to $\frac{8}{8}$?

   Ⓐ $\frac{0}{8}$ Ⓒ $\frac{6}{6}$

   Ⓑ $\frac{1}{8}$ Ⓓ $\frac{3}{6}$

4. Aaron is planting a vegetable garden. He made room in $\frac{1}{4}$ of his garden for beans. Which shape has a shaded part equivalent to $\frac{1}{4}$?

   Ⓐ 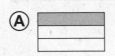   Ⓒ

   Ⓑ   Ⓓ

5. Danielle's model shows $\frac{1}{2} = \frac{2}{4}$. Describe a different way you could circle equal groups to show another equivalent fraction. Explain how you know your fraction is equivalent to $\frac{1}{2}$ and $\frac{2}{4}$.

_____

_____

_____

Number and Operations—Fractions

1. Which numbers from the number line are equal?

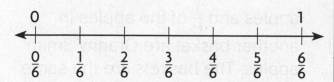

Ⓐ $\frac{6}{6}$ and 1   Ⓒ $\frac{0}{6}$ and 1

Ⓑ $\frac{3}{6}$ and $\frac{6}{6}$ Ⓓ $\frac{0}{6}$ and $\frac{6}{6}$

2. Cora cuts the apple pies into equal parts.

What fraction greater than 1 names both apple pies?

Ⓐ $\frac{2}{6}$ Ⓒ $\frac{6}{6}$

Ⓑ $\frac{6}{12}$ Ⓓ $\frac{12}{6}$

3. Emma colored some shapes. What fraction greater than 1 names the parts that she shaded?

Ⓐ $\frac{6}{2}$ Ⓒ $\frac{2}{3}$

Ⓑ $\frac{6}{3}$ Ⓓ $\frac{2}{6}$

4. Mr. Angelo sliced two pizzas into equal parts.

What fraction greater than 1 names both pizzas?

Ⓐ $\frac{2}{16}$ Ⓒ $\frac{16}{8}$

Ⓑ $\frac{8}{16}$ Ⓓ $\frac{16}{4}$

5. Greg painted three circles. He wrote the fraction $\frac{3}{24}$ for the shaded parts.

Is Greg correct? Explain your answer.

_____

_____

_____

Number and Operations–Fractions

1. Bill used $\frac{1}{3}$ cup of raisins and $\frac{2}{3}$ cup of banana chips to make a snack. Which statement correctly compares the fractions?

   Ⓐ $\frac{1}{3} > \frac{2}{3}$ Ⓒ $\frac{2}{3} > \frac{1}{3}$

   Ⓑ $\frac{2}{3} < \frac{1}{3}$ Ⓓ $\frac{2}{3} = \frac{1}{3}$

2. Mavis mixed $\frac{1}{4}$ quart of red paint with $\frac{3}{4}$ quart of yellow paint to make orange paint. Which of the following statements is **true**?

   Ⓐ Mavis used less yellow paint than red paint.

   Ⓑ Mavis used more red paint than yellow paint.

   Ⓒ Mavis used equal amounts of red and yellow paint.

   Ⓓ Mavis used more yellow paint than red paint.

3. Carlos found that $\frac{1}{2}$ of the apples in one basket are Granny Smith apples and $\frac{1}{6}$ of the apples in another basket are Granny Smith apples. The baskets are the same size. Which statement correctly compares the fractions?

   Ⓐ $\frac{1}{2} = \frac{1}{6}$ Ⓒ $\frac{1}{2} > \frac{1}{6}$

   Ⓑ $\frac{1}{2} < \frac{1}{6}$ Ⓓ $\frac{1}{6} > \frac{1}{2}$

4. Of the stars on the Monroe Elementary School flag, $\frac{2}{4}$ are gold and $\frac{2}{8}$ are black. Which statement correctly compares the fractions?

   Ⓐ $\frac{2}{8} > \frac{2}{4}$ Ⓒ $\frac{2}{4} = \frac{2}{8}$

   Ⓑ $\frac{2}{8} < \frac{2}{4}$ Ⓓ $\frac{2}{4} < \frac{2}{8}$

5. Tess ate $\frac{3}{8}$ of her granola bar. Gino ate $\frac{3}{4}$ of his granola bar. Both granola bars were the same size. Who ate more? Describe how you could use fraction strips to solve the problem.

_____

_____

_____

Number and Operations—Fractions

1. Dan and David are on the track team. Dan runs $\frac{1}{4}$ mile each day. David runs $\frac{3}{4}$ mile each day. Which statement is correct?

   (A) David runs farther than Dan each day.

   (B) David runs more than 1 mile each day.

   (C) David runs the same distance as Dan each day.

   (D) Dan runs farther than David each day.

2. Isabel and Raul are playing a game with fraction circles. Which statement is correct?

   (A) $\frac{1}{3} > \frac{2}{3}$ (C) $\frac{2}{3} < \frac{1}{3}$

   (B) $\frac{2}{3} = \frac{1}{3}$ (D) $\frac{2}{3} > \frac{1}{3}$

3. Chun lives $\frac{3}{8}$ mile from the library. Gail lives $\frac{5}{8}$ mile from the library. Which statement is correct?

   (A) Chun lives more than 1 mile from the library.

   (B) Chun lives farther from the library than Gail.

   (C) Gail lives farther from the library than Chun.

   (D) Gail and Chun live the same distance from the library.

4. Students are making quilt squares. They want $\frac{2}{6}$ of the quilt squares to be red and $\frac{4}{6}$ of the quilt squares to be white. Which statement correctly compares the fractions?

   (A) $\frac{2}{6} = \frac{4}{6}$ (C) $\frac{4}{6} < \frac{2}{6}$

   (B) $\frac{2}{6} < \frac{4}{6}$ (D) $\frac{2}{6} > \frac{4}{6}$

5. Kevin and Trevor each have a small pizza. Kevin eats $\frac{5}{6}$ of his pizza and Trevor eats $\frac{4}{6}$ of his pizza. Who eats the lesser amount? Explain how to use fraction circles to compare the fractions.

   _____

   _____

   _____

Number and Operations—Fractions

1. Jenna ate $\frac{1}{8}$ of one pizza. Mark ate $\frac{1}{6}$ of another pizza. The pizzas are the same size. Which statement correctly compares the amount of pizza that was eaten?

    Ⓐ $\frac{1}{6} < \frac{1}{8}$ Ⓒ $\frac{1}{8} > \frac{1}{6}$

    Ⓑ $\frac{1}{8} = \frac{1}{6}$ Ⓓ $\frac{1}{8} < \frac{1}{6}$

2. Jacob and Ella are reading the same book. Jacob read $\frac{5}{8}$ of the book. Ella read $\frac{5}{6}$ of the book. Which statement is correct?

    Ⓐ Jacob read more of the book than Ella.

    Ⓑ Ella read less of the book than Jacob.

    Ⓒ Jacob read less of the book than Ella.

    Ⓓ Ella and Jacob read the same amount of the book.

3. In a survey, $\frac{1}{3}$ of the students chose soccer as their favorite sport and $\frac{1}{4}$ chose basketball. Which statement correctly compares the fractions?

    Ⓐ $\frac{1}{3} < \frac{1}{4}$ Ⓒ $\frac{1}{3} > \frac{1}{4}$

    Ⓑ $\frac{1}{3} = \frac{1}{4}$ Ⓓ $\frac{1}{4} > \frac{1}{3}$

4. Maria put $\frac{3}{4}$ yard of fringe around the pillow she made. Nancy put $\frac{3}{8}$ yard of fringe around her pillow. Which statement correctly compares the fractions?

    Ⓐ $\frac{3}{4} > \frac{3}{8}$

    Ⓑ $\frac{3}{4} < \frac{3}{8}$

    Ⓒ $\frac{3}{4} = \frac{3}{8}$

    Ⓓ $\frac{3}{8} > \frac{3}{4}$

5. Rory can either have $\frac{2}{6}$ of a cheese pizza or $\frac{2}{8}$ of a vegetable pizza. The pizzas are the same size. Rory wants to eat the smaller amount of pizza. Which type of pizza should Rory eat? Explain your answer.

    _____

    _____

    _____

    _____

Number and Operations—Fractions

1. Floyd caught a fish that weighed $\frac{3}{4}$ pound. Kevin caught a fish that weighed $\frac{2}{3}$ pound. Which statement is correct?

   Ⓐ $\frac{3}{4} > \frac{2}{3}$

   Ⓑ $\frac{3}{4} < \frac{2}{3}$

   Ⓒ $\frac{2}{3} = \frac{3}{4}$

   Ⓓ $\frac{2}{3} > \frac{3}{4}$

2. There are two nature walks around the park. One trail is $\frac{7}{8}$ mile long. The other trail is $\frac{4}{8}$ mile long. Which statement is correct?

   Ⓐ $\frac{7}{8} < \frac{4}{8}$

   Ⓑ $\frac{7}{8} = \frac{4}{8}$

   Ⓒ $\frac{4}{8} < \frac{7}{8}$

   Ⓓ $\frac{4}{8} > \frac{7}{8}$

3. Olga is making play dough. She starts by mixing $\frac{1}{8}$ cup of salt with $\frac{1}{3}$ cup of water. Which statement is correct?

   Ⓐ $\frac{1}{8} = \frac{1}{3}$

   Ⓑ $\frac{1}{8} < \frac{1}{3}$

   Ⓒ $\frac{1}{8} > \frac{1}{3}$

   Ⓓ $\frac{1}{3} < \frac{1}{8}$

4. Kyle and Kelly planted seedlings. Kyle's plant is $\frac{5}{6}$ inch tall. Kelly's plant is $\frac{5}{8}$ inch tall. Which statement is correct?

   Ⓐ $\frac{5}{8} > \frac{5}{6}$

   Ⓑ $\frac{5}{8} = \frac{5}{6}$

   Ⓒ $\frac{5}{6} < \frac{5}{8}$

   Ⓓ $\frac{5}{6} > \frac{5}{8}$

5. Lynne and Crosby are meeting at the school playground. Lynne lives $\frac{4}{5}$ mile from the playground. Crosby lives $\frac{5}{6}$ mile from the playground. Who lives closer to the playground? Explain how you found your answer.

   _____

   _____

   _____

   _____

Number and Operations—Fractions

1. Pat, Elina, and Mike are meeting at the library. Pat lives $\frac{3}{4}$ mile from the library. Elina lives $\frac{1}{4}$ mile from the library. Mike lives $\frac{2}{4}$ mile from the library. Which list orders the fractions from **least** to **greatest**?

   Ⓐ $\frac{2}{4}, \frac{1}{4}, \frac{3}{4}$ Ⓒ $\frac{1}{4}, \frac{2}{4}, \frac{3}{4}$

   Ⓑ $\frac{1}{4}, \frac{3}{4}, \frac{2}{4}$ Ⓓ $\frac{3}{4}, \frac{2}{4}, \frac{1}{4}$

2. Ming is painting a picture. He has $\frac{2}{3}$ pint of red paint, $\frac{2}{8}$ pint of yellow paint, and $\frac{2}{6}$ pint of green paint. Which list orders the fractions from **greatest** to **least**?

   Ⓐ $\frac{2}{3}, \frac{2}{8}, \frac{2}{6}$ Ⓒ $\frac{2}{8}, \frac{2}{6}, \frac{2}{3}$

   Ⓑ $\frac{2}{3}, \frac{2}{6}, \frac{2}{8}$ Ⓓ $\frac{2}{6}, \frac{2}{3}, \frac{2}{8}$

3. Brian is making coconut bars. He needs $\frac{1}{3}$ cup coconut flakes, $\frac{1}{4}$ cup milk, and $\frac{1}{2}$ cup flour. Which list orders the fractions from **least** to **greatest**?

   Ⓐ $\frac{1}{4}, \frac{1}{3}, \frac{1}{2}$ Ⓒ $\frac{1}{4}, \frac{1}{2}, \frac{1}{3}$

   Ⓑ $\frac{1}{2}, \frac{1}{3}, \frac{1}{4}$ Ⓓ $\frac{1}{3}, \frac{1}{4}, \frac{1}{2}$

4. Cora measures the heights of three plants. The first plant is $\frac{4}{4}$ foot tall. The second plant is $\frac{4}{8}$ foot tall. The third plant is $\frac{4}{6}$ foot tall. Which list orders the fractions from **greatest** to **least**?

   Ⓐ $\frac{4}{4}, \frac{4}{6}, \frac{4}{8}$ Ⓒ $\frac{4}{8}, \frac{4}{6}, \frac{4}{4}$

   Ⓑ $\frac{4}{6}, \frac{4}{8}, \frac{4}{4}$ Ⓓ $\frac{4}{4}, \frac{4}{8}, \frac{4}{6}$

5. Gina measured the heights of three seedlings. The heights were $\frac{3}{8}$ inch, $\frac{3}{4}$ inch, and $\frac{3}{6}$ inch. Explain how Gina can compare and order the heights, from least to greatest, of the seedlings she measured.

   _____

   _____

   _____

   _____

   _____

Number and Operations—Fractions

1. Brad looked at the clock on his way to football practice.

What time is shown on Brad's clock?

Ⓐ thirteen minutes before nine

Ⓑ thirteen minutes after nine

Ⓒ nine forty-five

Ⓓ thirteen minutes before ten

2. Sarah looked at her watch before she began mowing the grass. The hour hand was between the 9 and the 10. The minute hand was on the 7. At what time did Sarah begin mowing the grass?

Ⓐ 7:09   Ⓒ 9:07

Ⓑ 7:10   Ⓓ 9:35

3. Chris looked at his watch before he began raking the leaves. The hour hand was between the 10 and the 11. The minute hand was on the 5. At what time did Chris begin raking the leaves?

Ⓐ 10:25   Ⓒ 5:11

Ⓑ 10:05   Ⓓ 5:10

4. Jillian checked the clock before she began piano practice.

What time is shown on Jillian's clock?

Ⓐ four twenty-five

Ⓑ twenty-seven minutes after four

Ⓒ three minutes before five

Ⓓ twenty-seven minutes before five

5. What time is it on a clock when the two hands form a straight line between 12 and 6? Explain.

_____

_____

_____

Measurement and Data

1. Keisha is eating dinner at quarter after 6:00. At what time is Keisha eating dinner?

   Ⓐ 5:45 A.M.

   Ⓑ 6:15 A.M.

   Ⓒ 5:45 P.M.

   Ⓓ 6:15 P.M.

2. Terry went fishing at 6 minutes past 7:00 in the morning. At what time did Terry go fishing?

   Ⓐ 6:07 A.M.

   Ⓑ 7:06 A.M.

   Ⓒ 6:07 P.M.

   Ⓓ 7:06 P.M.

3. Ricardo wakes up at quarter to 7:00 in the morning. At what time does Ricardo wake up?

   Ⓐ 6:45 A.M.

   Ⓑ 7:15 A.M.

   Ⓒ 6:45 P.M.

   Ⓓ 7:15 P.M.

4. Makati's class begins social studies at 10 minutes after 1:00 in the afternoon. At what time does social studies begin?

   Ⓐ 1:10 A.M.

   Ⓑ 10:01 A.M.

   Ⓒ 1:10 P.M.

   Ⓓ 10:01 P.M.

5. Charlie has a guitar lesson at 2:00. Is that time likely to be A.M. or P.M.? Explain.

   _____

   _____

   _____

   _____

   _____

Measurement and Data

1. Arianna started reading her book at 11:20 A.M. and stopped reading her book at 11:43 A.M. For how long did Arianna read her book?

   Ⓐ 23 minutes

   Ⓑ 28 minutes

   Ⓒ 33 minutes

   Ⓓ 63 minutes

2. Hector left to take a walk at 6:25 P.M. He returned home at 6:51 P.M. How long was Hector's walk?

   Ⓐ 16 minutes

   Ⓑ 21 minutes

   Ⓒ 26 minutes

   Ⓓ 76 minutes

3. Victoria started her spelling homework at 4:25 P.M. and finished at 4:37 P.M. How long did it take Victoria to complete her spelling homework?

   Ⓐ 27 minutes

   Ⓑ 22 minutes

   Ⓒ 17 minutes

   Ⓓ 12 minutes

4. Cheung started playing basketball at 9:17 A.M. He stopped playing at 9:45 A.M. How long did Cheung play basketball?

   Ⓐ 28 minutes   Ⓒ 38 minutes

   Ⓑ 32 minutes   Ⓓ 42 minutes

5. Magda worked on a computer from 1:40 P.M. to 2:14 P.M. Explain how you know whether she worked on the computer for more or less than 30 minutes.

   _____

   _____

   _____

   _____

Measurement and Data

1. Jai's piano lesson started at 4:35 P.M. The lesson lasted 45 minutes. What time did Jai's piano lesson end?

   (A) 3:50 P.M.

   (B) 5:10 P.M.

   (C) 5:20 P.M.

   (D) 5:35 P.M.

2. Ky was at the skateboard park for 35 minutes. He left the park at 3:10 P.M. What time did Ky arrive at the skateboard park?

   (A) 2:35 P.M.

   (B) 2:40 P.M.

   (C) 2:45 P.M.

   (D) 3:45 P.M.

3. A batch of muffins needs to bake for 22 minutes. Wade puts the muffins in the oven at 10:17 A.M. At what time should Wade take the muffins out of the oven?

   (A) 10:29 A.M.

   (B) 10:39 A.M.

   (C) 10:49 A.M.

   (D) 10:55 A.M.

4. Yul's art class started at 11:25 A.M. The class lasted 30 minutes. At what time did Yul's art class end?

   (A) 10:55 A.M.

   (B) 11:35 A.M.

   (C) 11:50 A.M.

   (D) 11:55 A.M.

5. Delia started her project at 9:30 A.M. and finished at 10:10 A.M. Colin finished his project at 10:45 A.M. Both students worked for the same amount of time. What time did Colin start his project? Explain how you know.

   _____

   _____

   _____

1. Omar rode his bike in the park for 45 minutes and rode in his neighborhood for 25 minutes. Omar stopped riding his bike at 4:40 P.M.

At what time did Omar start riding his bike?

Ⓐ 4:15 P.M.   Ⓒ 3:40 P.M.

Ⓑ 3:55 P.M.   Ⓓ 3:30 P.M.

2. Sophia folded laundry for 25 minutes. After folding laundry, she worked on a puzzle for 42 minutes. Sophia began folding laundry at 8:20 A.M. At what time did Sophia stop working on the puzzle?

Ⓐ 7:13 A.M.   Ⓒ 9:27 A.M.

Ⓑ 9:02 A.M.   Ⓓ 9:32 A.M.

3. Cheerleading practice started at 3:10 P.M. During practice, Dina practiced tumbling for 15 minutes. Then she practiced cheers for 35 minutes.

At what time did Dina's cheerleading practice end?

Ⓐ 3:25 P.M.   Ⓒ 4:00 P.M.

Ⓑ 3:45 P.M.   Ⓓ 4:15 P.M.

4. Mr. Carver spent 45 minutes making dinner. Then, he spent 18 minutes eating dinner. He finished eating at 6:15 P.M. At what time did Mr. Carver start making dinner?

Ⓐ 5:12 P.M.   Ⓒ 5:30 P.M.

Ⓑ 5:22 P.M.   Ⓓ 6:12 P.M.

5. Karl did his chores for 25 minutes. Then he read for 15 minutes. He finished reading at 5:20 P.M. Explain how you can find the time he began his chores.

_____

_____

_____

Measurement and Data

1. There are four bottles of punch on a shelf. The bottles are all the same size. Which bottle has the least amount of punch?

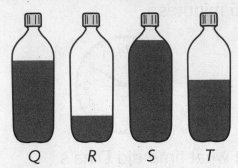

Q   R   S   T

Ⓐ Bottle Q   Ⓒ Bottle S

Ⓑ Bottle R   Ⓓ Bottle T

2. Meiki fills a mug with hot cocoa. Which is the best estimate of how much she poured into the mug?

Ⓐ about 1 liter

Ⓑ less than 1 liter

Ⓒ more than 1 liter

Ⓓ about 5 liters

3. There are four bottles of juice on the counter. The bottles are all the same size. Which bottle has the greatest amount of juice?

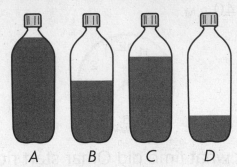

A   B   C   D

Ⓐ Bottle A   Ⓒ Bottle C

Ⓑ Bottle B   Ⓓ Bottle D

4. Jed fills a bucket with water to wash the floor. Which is the best estimate of how much water he put in the bucket?

Ⓐ a lot less than a liter

Ⓑ a little less than a liter

Ⓒ about a liter

Ⓓ more than a liter

5. A soup pot and a water bottle are the same height. Which one will hold more liquid? Explain.

_____

_____

_____

_____

Measurement and Data

1. Ling uses grams to measure the mass of an object in her room. Which object would be **best** measured using grams?

Ⓐ

Ⓑ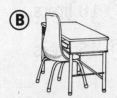

Ⓒ

Ⓓ

2. Kylie wants to find the mass of a pair of her sneakers. Which unit should she use?

Ⓐ liter   Ⓒ inch

Ⓑ kilogram   Ⓓ gram

3. Jason uses a balance to compare the masses of the objects shown. What is true about the objects?

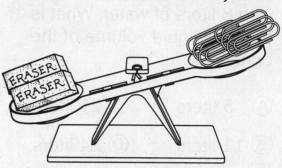

Ⓐ The mass of the erasers is the same as the mass of the paper clips.

Ⓑ The mass of the erasers is less than the mass of the paper clips.

Ⓒ The mass of the paper clips is less than the mass of the erasers.

Ⓓ The mass of the paper clips is greater than the mass of the erasers.

4. Stav adopted a puppy. The data sheet for the puppy gave its mass as 2, but left off the unit. What unit makes sense? Explain your thinking.

_____

_____

_____

_____

Measurement and Data

1. Bryce has a container completely filled with 13 liters of water. Ben has a container completely filled with 8 liters of water. What is the total liquid volume of the containers?

   Ⓐ 5 liters   Ⓒ 21 liters

   Ⓑ 11 liters   Ⓓ 24 liters

2. An online company shipped three packages. The packages had masses of 8 kilograms, 15 kilograms, and 9 kilograms. What is the total mass of the three packages?

   Ⓐ 23 kilograms

   Ⓑ 24 kilograms

   Ⓒ 32 kilograms

   Ⓓ 34 kilograms

3. Mama's Restaurant sold a total of 15 liters of orange juice in 3 hours. The same amount of orange juice was sold each hour. How many liters of orange juice were sold each hour?

   Ⓐ 5 liters   Ⓒ 18 liters

   Ⓑ 12 liters   Ⓓ 45 liters

4. Simon pours 19 liters of water into one bucket and 15 liters of water into another bucket. Each bucket is filled completely. What is the total liquid volume of the two buckets?

   Ⓐ 4 liters

   Ⓑ 14 liters

   Ⓒ 24 liters

   Ⓓ 34 liters

5. At a football game, the Pep Club sold a total of 18 liters of fruit punch in 2 hours. The same amount of fruit punch was sold each hour. Explain how to find the amount of fruit punch that was sold each hour.

   _____

   _____

   _____

   _____

Use the table for 1–2.

Mike asked people what season they liked best. The tally table shows the results.

Favorite Season	
Winter	卌 III
Spring	卌 卌 I
Summer	IIII
Fall	卌

1. How many people chose Winter or Summer?

   Ⓐ 4   Ⓒ 11

   Ⓑ 10   Ⓓ 12

2. How many **more** students chose Spring than Fall?

   Ⓐ 4   Ⓒ 6

   Ⓑ 5   Ⓓ 11

Use the table for 3–4.

Rory and his classmates voted for a favorite class activity. They organized the data in a tally table.

Favorite Class Activity	
Science Fair	卌 卌
Bake Sale	IIII
Fitness Fun Day	卌 卌 II
Class Play	卌 IIII

3. How many students chose the Science Fair or Fitness Fun Day?

   Ⓐ 6   Ⓒ 20

   Ⓑ 12   Ⓓ 22

4. How many **fewer** students chose a Bake Sale than Fitness Fun Day?

   Ⓐ 4   Ⓒ 10

   Ⓑ 8   Ⓓ 12

5. Dan asked 24 members of his class how they traveled to their last vacation spot. The frequency table shows the results. Complete the table and explain how you did it.

Travel Vehicle	Boys	Girls
Car		4
Airplane	6	5
Bus	2	3

_____

_____

_____

1. Ms. Sanchez's class took pictures of a lighthouse during a field trip. The picture graph shows how many pictures each student took.

Lighthouse Pictures	
Gerald	📷 📷 📷 📷 📷 📷 📷
Yung	📷 📷 📷 📷 📷 📷
Ramesh	📷 📷
Jose	📷 📷 📷 📷 📷 📷 📷 📷 📷 📷
Key: Each 📷 = 2 pictures.	

How many pictures were taken in all?

Ⓐ 28   Ⓒ 52

Ⓑ 32   Ⓓ 56

2. The picture graph shows the number of bottles Mr. Tao's class recycled each week for an Earth Day project.

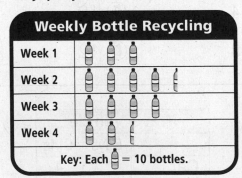

Weekly Bottle Recycling	
Week 1	
Week 2	
Week 3	
Week 4	
Key: Each 🍶 = 10 bottles.	

How many bottles were recycled during Week 2 and Week 3?

Ⓐ 9   Ⓒ 85

Ⓑ 14   Ⓓ 140

3. Mrs. Hampton's class made a picture graph to show the type of material used to make each picture at an art show.

Pictures at the Art Show	
Chalk	▌ ▌ ▌ ▌ ▌ ▌
Crayon	▌ ▌ ▌ ▌ ▏
Paint	▌ ▌ ▌ ▌ ▌ ▌ ▌
Key: Each ▌ = 2 pictures.	

How many **fewer** pictures were made with crayon than with paint?

Ⓐ 4   Ⓒ 9

Ⓑ 5   Ⓓ 12

4. Pam tossed a coin 20 times and made a picture graph of her data.

Coin Toss Results	
Heads	○ ○ ○ ○
Tails	○ ○ ○ ○ ○ ○
Key: Each ○ = 2 coin tosses.	

Explain how the picture graph would be different if each circle represented 4 coin tosses.

_____

_____

_____

_____

Measurement and Data

Use the table for 1–2.

Kim did a survey to learn which pet her classmates liked best. She wrote the results in a table and will use the data to make a picture graph with a key of ☺ = 3 students.

Favorite Pet

Kind of Pet	Number of Students
Goldfish	12
Bird	15

1. How many ☺ will Kim draw for Goldfish?

   Ⓐ 2   Ⓑ 3   Ⓒ 4   Ⓓ 5

2. How many ☺ will Kim draw for Birds?

   Ⓐ 2   Ⓑ 3   Ⓒ 4   Ⓓ 5

3. Jerel made a picture graph to show the number of sunny days his city had in June and July. This is the key to Jerel's picture graph.

   Key: Each ☼ **= 10 days.**

   How many sunny days do ☼ ☼ ☼ ☼ stand for?

   Ⓐ 3   Ⓒ 30
   Ⓑ 4   Ⓓ 35

4. Jamie saw 24 red cars and 16 blue cars. She made a picture graph to show her results. If △ = 4 cars, how many △s show the number of blue cars she saw?

   Ⓐ 4   Ⓒ 8
   Ⓑ 5   Ⓓ 16

5. Jeff took a survey about the snack his 26 classmates liked best. He used the data to begin making a picture graph. Complete Jeff's picture graph. Explain your work.

Favorite Snack	
Crackers	☺ ☺ ☺ ☺
Fruit	
Key: Each ☺ = 4 students.	

_____

_____

_____

Measurement and Data

Use the graph for 1–3.

Carrie asked people at the mall to choose a favorite type of music. The bar graph shows the results.

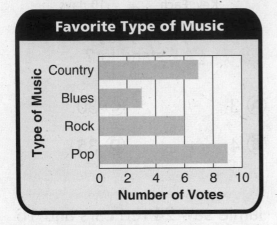

Favorite Type of Music

Type of Music: Country, Blues, Rock, Pop
Number of Votes: 0 2 4 6 8 10

1. How many **more** people chose Rock than Blues?

   Ⓐ 2   Ⓒ 4

   Ⓑ 3   Ⓓ 9

2. How many people in all chose a type of music?

   Ⓐ 4   Ⓒ 22

   Ⓑ 16   Ⓓ 25

3. How many **more** people would have to choose Blues to have the same number of people choose Blues and Country?

   Ⓐ 3   Ⓒ 6

   Ⓑ 4   Ⓓ 7

4. Diego made a graph to show how many butterflies he saw in his yard each day. How many **fewer** butterflies did Diego see on Tuesday than on the day that he saw the most butterflies? Explain how you used the graph to find the answer.

Butterflies in the Garden

Number of Butterflies: 0 2 4 6 8 10 12 14
Day: Monday, Tuesday, Wednesday, Thursday, Friday

_____

_____

_____

_____

© Houghton Mifflin Harcourt Publishing Company

Use the table for 1–2.

Brendon wants to use a table with data about the number of oranges picked to make a bar graph.

Oranges Picked

Type of Orange	Bushels
Navel	15
Pineapple	12
Temple	10
Valencia	14

1. How many bars will Brendon have on his graph?

   Ⓐ 2 Ⓒ 9

   Ⓑ 4 Ⓓ 16

2. Which type of orange will have the longest bar?

   Ⓐ Navel

   Ⓑ Pineapple

   Ⓒ Temple

   Ⓓ Valencia

3. Joey is making a bar graph to show how many pets his classmates have. Which pet will have the shortest bar in his graph?

   Ⓐ 8 cats Ⓒ 4 dogs

   Ⓑ 6 hamsters Ⓓ 3 horses

4. Martina is making a bar graph to show the 37 finches she saw in her garden from Monday through Friday. How tall should Martina make the bar to show how many finches she saw on Wednesday? Explain your answer and complete the graph.

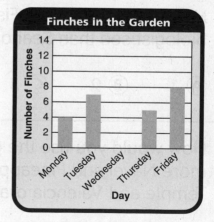

_____

_____

_____

_____

_____

Use the graph for 1–2.

A biologist made a bar graph to show how many samples of each type of marine life she saw on a dive.

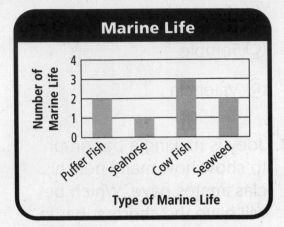

1. Of which type of marine life did the marine biologist see the **fewest**?

Ⓐ Cow Fish   Ⓒ Seahorse

Ⓑ Puffer Fish   Ⓓ Seaweed

2. How many more Cow Fish did the biologist see than Seahorses?

Ⓐ 1   Ⓑ 2   Ⓒ 3   Ⓓ 4

Use the graph for 3–4.

Nigel made a bar graph to show how many bushels of each type of orange are for sale at a fruit stand.

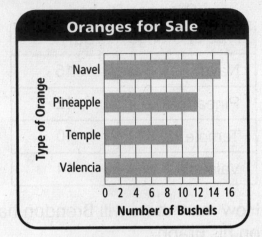

3. How many **more** bushels of Pineapple oranges and Navel oranges are there than Temple oranges and Valencia oranges?

Ⓐ 1 bushel

Ⓑ 3 bushels

Ⓒ 7 bushels

Ⓓ 24 bushels

4. How would you use the graph to find out if there were more Navel and Pineapple oranges for sale or more Temple and Valencia oranges for sale?

_____

_____

_____

_____

Measurement and Data

Use the line plot for 1–2.

Mr. Robinson's students made a line plot to show the number of hats they each have.

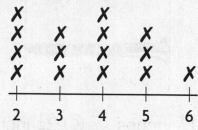

Number of Hats

1. How many students have 4 or fewer hats?

   Ⓐ 3   Ⓒ 7

   Ⓑ 4   Ⓓ 11

2. How many students were included in the line plot?

   Ⓐ 13   Ⓒ 15

   Ⓑ 14   Ⓓ 16

Use the line plot for 3–4.

Anna made a line plot to show the number of books each student in her class read for a reading contest.

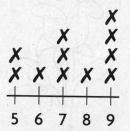

Number of Books Read

3. How many students read 9 books?

   Ⓐ 4   Ⓒ 2

   Ⓑ 3   Ⓓ 1

4. How many students read **fewer** than 8 books?

   Ⓐ 4   Ⓒ 6

   Ⓑ 5   Ⓓ 7

5. Lewis made a line plot to show the number of hours students in his class spend at practice each week. Find the total number of students and the total number of hours. Explain how you found your answers.

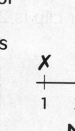 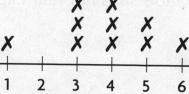

Number of Hours

_____

_____

_____

_____

Measurement and Data

1. Mrs. Williams uses an inch ruler to measure a flower in a picture. How tall is the flower to the nearest fourth inch?

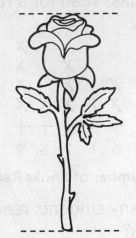

Ⓐ 2 inches   Ⓒ $2\frac{3}{4}$ inches

Ⓑ $2\frac{1}{4}$ inches   Ⓓ 3 inches

2. Hector uses an inch ruler to measure a screw. What is the length of the screw to the nearest half inch?

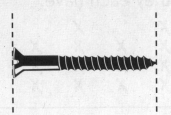

Ⓐ $1\frac{1}{2}$ inches   Ⓒ $2\frac{1}{2}$ inches

Ⓑ 2 inches   Ⓓ 3 inches

3. Julio uses an inch ruler to measure a pencil sharpener. What is the length of the pencil sharpener to the nearest fourth inch?

Ⓐ $\frac{1}{4}$ inch   Ⓒ 1 inch

Ⓑ $\frac{3}{4}$ inch   Ⓓ $1\frac{3}{4}$ inches

4. Jade says her hair clip is $2\frac{1}{4}$ inches long. Do you agree? Explain.

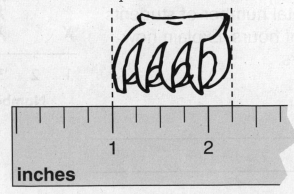

_____

_____

Measurement and Data

1. Greg drew the shape of the parking lot at school.

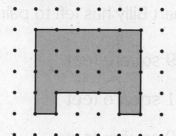

What is the area of the parking lot?

Ⓐ 15 square units

Ⓑ 17 square units

Ⓒ 20 square units

Ⓓ 22 square units

2. Mr. Chang wants to buy a rug for his living room. Which of the following does Mr. Chang need to find to know how much rug he will need?

Ⓐ height of the living room

Ⓑ length of the living room

Ⓒ perimeter of the living room

Ⓓ area of the living room

3. Sophia drew the shape of a path on dot paper.

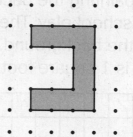

What is the area of the path Sophia drew?

Ⓐ   8 square units

Ⓑ   9 square units

Ⓒ 10 square units

Ⓓ 12 square units

4. Carmen needs to find the area for a project she is doing. Which could be Carmen's project?

Ⓐ gluing string around a picture

Ⓑ using wood to make a frame

Ⓒ painting a wall

Ⓓ putting a fence around a pool

5. The drawing shows the principal's office. Find the area of the principal's office and explain how you did it.

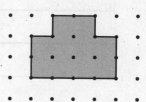

_____

_____

Measurement and Data

Use the information for 1–3.

Billy is painting the background for the school play. The diagram shows the background. Each unit square is 1 square foot.

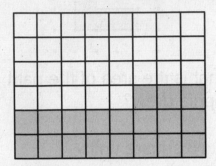

1. The shaded part shows the part Billy has already painted. What is the area of the background that Billy has already painted?

Ⓐ 16 square feet

Ⓑ 19 square feet

Ⓒ 22 square feet

Ⓓ 48 square feet

2. The white part shows the part Billy has left to paint. What is the area of the part Billy has left to paint?

Ⓐ 19 square feet

Ⓑ 21 square feet

Ⓒ 29 square feet

Ⓓ 32 square feet

3. What is the total area of the background that Billy is painting for the school play?

Ⓐ 28 square feet

Ⓑ 36 square feet

Ⓒ 40 square feet

Ⓓ 48 square feet

4. Naomi is putting square tiles on the floor of her bathroom. Each tile is 1 square foot. The diagram shows her bathroom. Find the area of the bathroom. Explain how you found the area.

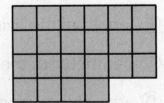

_____

_____

_____

Measurement and Data

1. The drawing shows Seth's plan for a footpath through his garden. Each unit square is 1 square foot. What is the area of Seth's footpath?

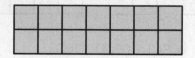

Ⓐ 14 square feet

Ⓑ 16 square feet

Ⓒ 18 square feet

Ⓓ 21 square feet

2. Keisha draws a sketch of a tile mosaic she wants to make on grid paper. Each unit square is 1 square inch. What is the area of Keisha's mosaic?

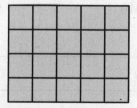

Ⓐ 9 square inches

Ⓑ 18 square inches

Ⓒ 20 square inches

Ⓓ 25 square inches

3. The drawing represents a vegetable garden in the Wilsons' backyard. Each unit square is 1 square meter. What is the area of the Wilsons' vegetable garden?

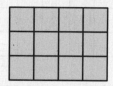

Ⓐ 7 square meters

Ⓑ 12 square meters

Ⓒ 14 square meters

Ⓓ 24 square meters

4. Roberto put square tiles down in the entryway. Each tile is 1 square foot. Write the area of the entryway floor. Explain how you found the area.

_____

_____

_____

_____

_____

_____

Measurement and Data

1. Brian drew these shapes. If the pattern continues, the next shape will have an area of 24 square units. What will be its length?

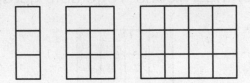

Ⓐ 4 units

Ⓑ 6 units

Ⓒ 8 units

Ⓓ 16 units

2. Brent uses carpet squares to make the pattern. Each unit square is 1 square foot. If the pattern continues, what will be the area of the fourth shape?

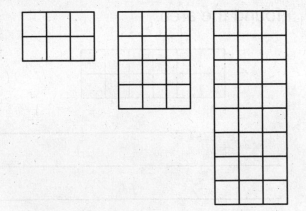

Ⓐ 27 square feet

Ⓑ 30 square feet

Ⓒ 42 square feet

Ⓓ 48 square feet

3. Julia uses tiles to make the pattern below. Each unit square is 1 square inch. If the pattern continues, what will be the area of the fourth shape?

Ⓐ 6 square inches

Ⓑ 8 square inches

Ⓒ 10 square inches

Ⓓ 12 square inches

4. Amy measured two rooms at her school. The first room is 8 feet wide and 10 feet long. The second room is 16 feet wide and 10 feet long. Describe how the lengths and widths of the rooms are related. Then use this information to explain how the areas of the two rooms are related.

_____

_____

_____

_____

_____

_____

_____

Measurement and Data

1. Colby drew a diagram of his garden. Each unit square is 1 square foot. What is the area of Colby's garden?

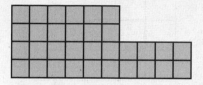

Ⓐ 32 square feet

Ⓑ 30 square feet

Ⓒ 24 square feet

Ⓓ 20 square feet

2. The school office is shown. Each unit square is equal to 1 square meter. What is the total area of the school office?

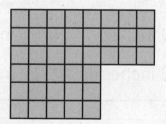

Ⓐ 24 square meters

Ⓑ 30 square meters

Ⓒ 39 square meters

Ⓓ 48 square meters

3. Mrs. McCarthy's art studio is shown. Each unit square is equal to 1 square meter. What is the total area of Mrs. McCarthy's art studio?

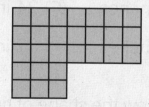

Ⓐ 35 square meters

Ⓑ 27 square meters

Ⓒ 25 square meters

Ⓓ 21 square meters

4. Jake drew the diagram of his bedroom shown. Each unit square is equal to 1 square meter. Write the area of Jake's bedroom. Explain the steps you used to find the area.

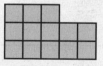

_____

_____

_____

_____

_____

_____

Measurement and Data

1. Irie draws a 4-sided shape on his paper that measures 8 inches on each side. What is the perimeter of the shape?

   (A) 8 inches   (C) 24 inches

   (B) 16 inches   (D) 32 inches

2. Yuko drew the shape of her garden on grid paper.

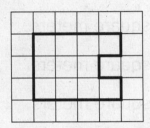

   What is the perimeter of Yuko's garden?

   (A) 14 units   (C) 16 units

   (B) 15 units   (D) 17 units

3. Adam drew this shape on grid paper.

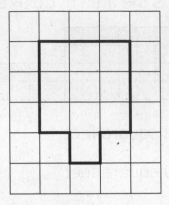

   What is the perimeter of the shape?

   (A) 14 units   (C) 10 units

   (B) 12 units   (D) 9 units

4. A shape has 4 sides. Two sides measure 5 inches and two sides measure 8 inches. What is the perimeter of the shape?

   (A) 40 inches   (C) 16 inches

   (B) 26 inches   (D) 10 inches

5. Ling drew the shape of a hopscotch game on grid paper. Write the perimeter of the shape. Explain how you found the perimeter.

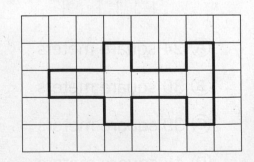

   _____

   _____

   _____

Measurement and Data

1. Fiona bought a picture with a perimeter of 24 inches. Which picture did she buy?

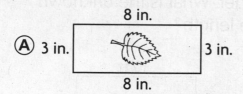

Ⓐ 3 in.   8 in. / 8 in.   3 in.

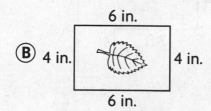

Ⓑ 4 in.   6 in. / 6 in.   4 in.

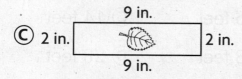

Ⓒ 2 in.   9 in. / 9 in.   2 in.

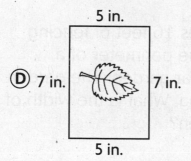

Ⓓ 7 in.   5 in. / 5 in.   7 in.

2. Kim wants to put trim around a picture she drew. How many centimeters of trim does Kim need for the perimeter of the picture?

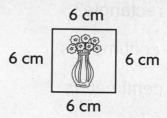

6 cm   6 cm / 6 cm   6 cm

Ⓐ 6 centimeters

Ⓑ 12 centimeters

Ⓒ 24 centimeters

Ⓓ 36 centimeters

3. Mr. Gasper is putting wood trim around this window. How many feet of wood trim does Mr. Gasper need for the perimeter of the window?

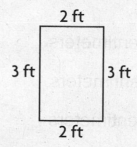

2 ft   3 ft / 3 ft   2 ft

Ⓐ 6 feet   Ⓒ 12 feet

Ⓑ 10 feet   Ⓓ 13 feet

4. Dylan used a centimeter ruler to draw this square. Find the perimeter of Dylan's square and explain how you did it.

_____

_____

1. Natasha cut out a rectangle that has a perimeter of 34 centimeters. The width of the rectangle is 7 centimeters. What is the length of the rectangle?

Ⓐ   5 centimeters

Ⓑ 10 centimeters

Ⓒ 20 centimeters

Ⓓ 27 centimeters

2. Vanessa uses a ruler to draw a square. The perimeter of the square is 12 centimeters. What is the length of each side of the square?

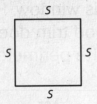

Ⓐ   3 centimeters

Ⓑ   4 centimeters

Ⓒ   6 centimeters

Ⓓ 48 centimeters

3. Mrs. Rios wants to put a wallpaper border around the room shown. She will use 36 feet of wallpaper border. What is the unknown side length?

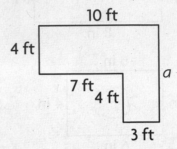

Ⓐ 6 feet   Ⓒ 14 feet

Ⓑ 8 feet   Ⓓ 28 feet

4. Frank uses 16 feet of fencing around the perimeter of a rectangular garden. The garden is 5 feet long. What is the width of the garden?

Ⓐ 11 feet

Ⓑ   6 feet

Ⓒ   3 feet

Ⓓ   2 feet

5. Mr. Rios has a rectangular rug. The perimeter of the rug is 28 feet. The width of the rug is 6 feet. Find the length of the rug. Explain the steps you used to find the missing length.

_____

_____

_____

Use the information for 1–3.

Sarah is building a garden in the backyard. She drew a diagram of one way to lay out the garden.

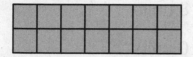

1. What is the perimeter of the garden?

   Ⓐ 9 units

   Ⓑ 12 units

   Ⓒ 14 units

   Ⓓ 18 units

2. What is the area of the garden?

   Ⓐ 6 square units

   Ⓑ 12 square units

   Ⓒ 14 square units

   Ⓓ 18 square units

3. Sarah wants her rectangular garden to have the greatest possible area, but she wants the same perimeter as shown in her diagram. Which could be the length and width of Sarah's garden?

   Ⓐ 5 units by 4 units

   Ⓑ 6 units by 3 units

   Ⓒ 8 units by 1 unit

   Ⓓ 5 units by 2 units

4. Kathy drew these rectangles on grid paper. Explain how the perimeters and areas of the rectangles are related.

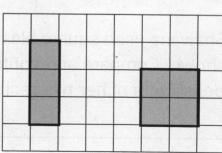

_____

_____

_____

_____

_____

Use the information for 1–3.

Cheung drew two rectangles on grid paper.

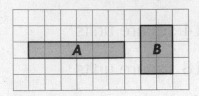

1. What is the area of each rectangle?

   Ⓐ A: Area = 6 square units;
      B: Area = 6 square units

   Ⓑ A: Area = 6 square units;
      B: Area = 3 square units

   Ⓒ A: Area = 14 square units;
      B: Area = 10 square units

   Ⓓ A: Area = 7 square units;
      B: Area = 5 square units

2. What is the perimeter of rectangle B?

   Ⓐ 5 units

   Ⓑ 6 units

   Ⓒ 8 units

   Ⓓ 10 units

3. Which statement about the perimeters and areas of Cheung's rectangles is true?

   Ⓐ The areas are the same and the perimeters are the same.

   Ⓑ The areas are the same and the perimeters are different.

   Ⓒ The areas are different and the perimeters are different.

   Ⓓ The areas are different and the perimeters are the same.

4. Shawana used square tiles to make the rectangles shown. Compare and contrast the areas and perimeters of her two rectangles.

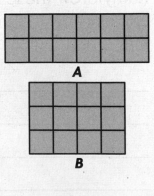

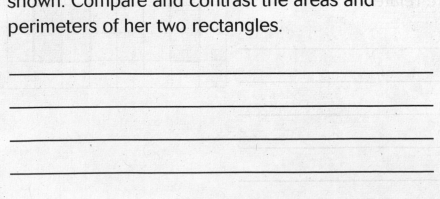

_____

_____

_____

_____

1. Abby drew a point. Which shows a point?

   Ⓐ •

   Ⓑ •————————•

   Ⓒ •————————▸

   Ⓓ ◂————————▸

2. Cyrus uses line segments to draw a shape.

   How many line segments does Cyrus's shape have?

   Ⓐ 6   Ⓒ 8

   Ⓑ 7   Ⓓ 9

3. Four friends draw shapes. Rachel, Zoe, and Jorge draw closed shapes. Andy draws an open shape. Which is Andy's shape?

   Ⓐ   Ⓒ

   Ⓑ    Ⓓ

4. Jamey drew this shape.

   What shape did Jamey draw?

   Ⓐ line

   Ⓑ line segment

   Ⓒ point

   Ⓓ ray

5. Randy drew these two shapes. Classify each shape as *open* or *closed,* and explain how you know.

   _____

   _____

   _____

   _____

1. How many right angles does this shape appear to have?

- (A) 0
- (C) 2
- (B) 1
- (D) 5

2. Look at the shape.

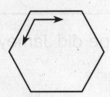

Which **best** describes the marked angle?

- (A) less than a right angle
- (B) greater than a right angle
- (C) a right angle
- (D) a straight angle

3. Which describes the angles of this triangle?

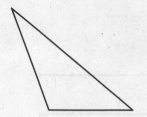

- (A) 1 greater than a right angle; 2 less than a right angle
- (B) 1 greater than a right angle; 2 right angles
- (C) 2 greater than a right angle; 1 less than a right angle
- (D) 1 greater than a right angle; 1 right angle; 1 less than a right angle

4. Which capital letter appears to have an angle that is less than a right angle?

- (A) H
- (C) T
- (B) L
- (D) Z

5. Mrs. Simpson drew this shape. Explain how to classify the marked angle.

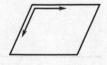

_____

_____

_____

_____

Geometry

1. Which shape is **not** a polygon?

Ⓐ 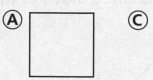   Ⓒ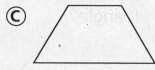

Ⓑ 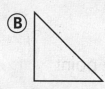   Ⓓ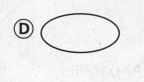

2. Vance drew a polygon with 6 sides. What is the name of the polygon he drew?

Ⓐ triangle

Ⓑ pentagon

Ⓒ hexagon

Ⓓ decagon

3. A builder is using tiles on a bathroom floor. Each tile has 8 angles. What type of polygon are the tiles?

Ⓐ decagon   Ⓒ octagon

Ⓑ hexagon   Ⓓ quadrilateral

4. Kendall drew one closed shape using 5 line segments. Which shape did Kendall draw?

Ⓐ quadrilateral

Ⓑ pentagon

Ⓒ hexagon

Ⓓ octagon

5. Alex drew these four shapes. Circle the shape that is **not** a polygon. Explain why the shape you circled is not a polygon.

_____

_____

_____

_____

1. How many pairs of parallel sides does this hexagon appear to have?

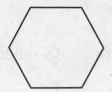

Ⓐ 0   Ⓒ 3

Ⓑ 1   Ⓓ 6

2. Brad drew a quadrilateral. Which sides of the quadrilateral appear to be parallel?

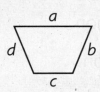

Ⓐ a and b   Ⓒ b and d

Ⓑ a and c   Ⓓ c and d

3. Which word can be used to describe the dashed sides of the triangle?

Ⓐ parallel   Ⓒ point

Ⓑ perpendicular Ⓓ quadrilateral

4. Sami uses straws to model a triangle. Which word can be used to describe the two dashed sides of the triangle?

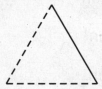

Ⓐ intersecting   Ⓒ perpendicular

Ⓑ parallel   Ⓓ right

5. Brenton and Katie made a model of a polygon. Brenton said the two dashed sides shown are parallel. Katie said they are intersecting. Who is correct? Explain.

_____
_____
_____
_____

1. Hillary drew this shape.

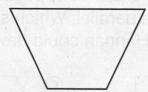

   Which word **best** describes the shape Hillary drew?

   Ⓐ square   Ⓒ rhombus

   Ⓑ rectangle   Ⓓ trapezoid

2. Cooper used toothpicks to make a shape.

   Which **best** describes the shape Cooper made?

   Ⓐ decagon   Ⓒ square

   Ⓑ open shape   Ⓓ trapezoid

3. Edward says he drew a quadrilateral. Which of these could **not** be Edward's shape?

   Ⓐ 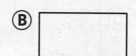   Ⓒ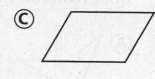

   Ⓑ    Ⓓ

4. Helen drew this shape.

   Which word **best** describes the shape Helen drew?

   Ⓐ rectangle   Ⓒ square

   Ⓑ rhombus   Ⓓ trapezoid

5. Aidan draws a shape with 4 sides of equal length and no right angles. Classify Aidan's shape using one or more of the following terms: *quadrilateral, rhombus, square, rectangle, trapezoid.* Explain how you classified the shape.

   _____

   _____

   _____

   _____

   _____

1. Melody draws a quadrilateral with 2 pairs of opposite sides that are parallel. Which could be the quadrilateral Melody draws?

Ⓐ   Ⓒ

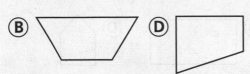

Ⓑ   Ⓓ

3. Hannah drew a quadrilateral with exactly 1 pair of opposite sides that are parallel. Which shows a shape Hannah could have drawn?

Ⓐ   Ⓒ

Ⓑ   Ⓓ

2. Gina drew a quadrilateral that has 4 sides of equal length and 4 right angles. Which shape did she draw?

Ⓐ pentagon   Ⓒ trapezoid

Ⓑ square   Ⓓ triangle

4. Henry drew a quadrilateral that has 2 pairs of sides of equal length and 4 right angles. Which shape did he draw?

Ⓐ hexagon   Ⓒ trapezoid

Ⓑ pentagon   Ⓓ rectangle

5. Josie drew a quadrilateral with exactly 1 pair of parallel sides. Draw and classify a quadrilateral that could be like Josie's. Explain why you drew what you drew.

_____

_____

_____

_____

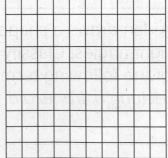

1. Which triangle appears to have 1 right angle and 0 sides of equal length?

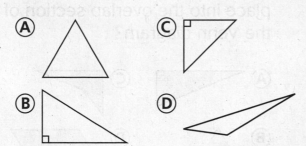

2. How are triangles *L*, *M*, and *N* alike?

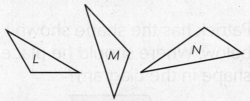

Ⓐ They all have 1 angle greater than a right angle.

Ⓑ They all have 1 right angle.

Ⓒ They all have 3 angles less than a right angle.

Ⓓ All of their sides are of equal length.

3. Ping drew a triangle that has 3 angles smaller than a right angle and 3 sides of equal length. Which shows Ping's triangle?

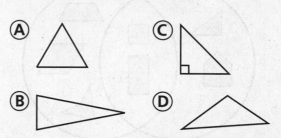

4. Brian drew a triangle that has 1 angle larger than a right angle and 0 sides of equal length. Which shows Brian's triangle?

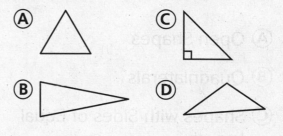

5. Caden made triangles *A*, *B*, and *C*. Compare the angles and side lengths of Caden's triangles.

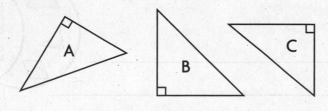

_____

_____

Use the Venn diagram for 1–3.

Polygons with Right Angles   **A**

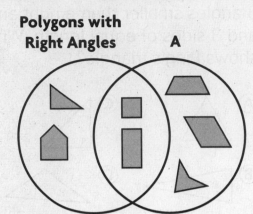

1. Patrick used the Venn diagram to sort shapes. Which label could he use for part A?

   (A) Open Shapes

   (B) Quadrilaterals

   (C) Shapes with Sides of Equal Length

   (D) Shapes with 1 Right Angle

2. Patrick found some more shapes to sort. Which shape should he place into the overlap section of the Venn diagram?

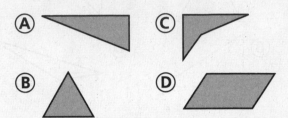

   (A)   (C)

   (B)   (D)

3. Patrick has the shape shown below. Where should he place the shape in the diagram?

   (A) part A

   (B) Polygons with Right Angles

   (C) overlap section

   (D) outside the Venn diagram

4. Kendra used a Venn diagram to sort shapes.

   Write a label she could use for circle A. Explain your reasoning.

   Quadrilaterals   A

   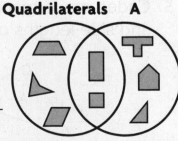

   _____

   _____

   _____

   _____

   _____

Geometry

1. Talon divides a square into equal parts that each show $\frac{1}{6}$. Which could be Talon's square?

Ⓐ 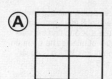   Ⓒ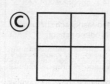

Ⓑ 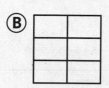   Ⓓ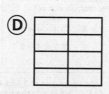

2. Colleen drew lines to divide a trapezoid into equal parts that each represent $\frac{1}{3}$ of the whole area. Which could be Colleen's trapezoid?

Ⓐ

Ⓑ

Ⓒ

Ⓓ

3. Tad divides a rhombus into equal parts that each show $\frac{1}{2}$. Which could be Tad's rhombus?

Ⓐ 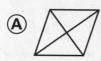   Ⓒ

Ⓑ    Ⓓ

4. Dennie drew lines to divide a shape into 3 parts each with equal area. Which could be Dennie's shape?

Ⓐ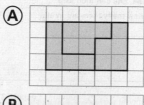

Ⓑ

Ⓒ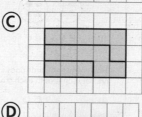

Ⓓ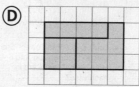

5. Reese divided the shaded shape into equal parts. Write the unit fraction that names each part of the divided whole. Explain your reasoning.

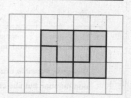

_____

_____

Geometry

Name _____

1. There are 5 tables in the library. Four students are sitting at each table.

How many students are sitting in the library?

Ⓐ 9   Ⓒ **20**

Ⓑ 16   Ⓓ 24

2. Alondra made 3 bracelets. There are 7 beads on each bracelet.

How many beads did Alondra use to make the bracelets?

Ⓐ 10   Ⓒ **21**

Ⓑ 14   Ⓓ 24

3. Stella decorated using 4 groups of balloons. She drew this model to show the number of balloons.

How many balloons did Stella use to decorate?

Ⓐ 3   Ⓒ 9

Ⓑ 6   Ⓓ **12**

4. Mrs. Bennett sorted spools of thread into 3 containers. Each container held 3 spools.

How many spools of thread does Mrs. Bennett have in all?

Ⓐ 6   Ⓒ 10

Ⓑ **9**   Ⓓ 12

5. Cory, Greg, and Carrie each have 4 stickers. Carrie says that she can find how many stickers they have in all by drawing 3 equal groups. How can she use the equal groups to find the number of stickers in all?

Carrie should draw 3 groups of 4. She can then skip

count by 4 three times to find how many there are in all.

There are 12 stickers in all.

Name _____

1. Eric was doing his math homework. Eric wrote:

$2 + 2 + 2 + 2 + 2$

Which is another way to show what Eric wrote?

Ⓐ 2×2 Ⓒ 10×2

Ⓑ 5×2 Ⓓ $5 + 2$

2. Dallas and Mark each sharpened 4 pencils before school.

Which sentence shows the number of pencils sharpened in all?

Ⓐ $2 + 2 = 4$ Ⓒ $4 \times 4 = 16$

Ⓑ $4 + 2 = 6$ Ⓓ $2 \times 4 = 8$

3. A pet store has some fish bowls on display. There are 3 fish in each of 5 bowls. Which number sentence shows how many fish there are in all?

Ⓐ $5 \times 3 = 15$ Ⓒ $5 + 3 = 8$

Ⓑ $5 \times 5 = 25$ Ⓓ $3 \times 3 = 9$

4. Carlos spent 5 minutes working on each of 8 math problems. He can use 8×5 to find the total number of minutes he spent on the problems. Which is equal to 8×5?

Ⓐ $8 + 5$

Ⓑ $8 + 8 + 8$

Ⓒ $5 + 5 + 5 + 5$

Ⓓ $5 + 5 + 5 + 5 + 5 + 5 + 5 + 5$

5. Ryan bought 4 packages of 3 juice boxes each. Write a multiplication and an addition sentence to show how many juice boxes Ryan bought in all. Explain how your number sentences represent the problem. **$4 \times 3 = 12$; Possible explanation: the factor 4 stands for the 4 packages and the factor**

3 stands for the number of juice boxes in each package. The product,

12, represents the total number of juice boxes.

$3 + 3 + 3 + 3 = 12$; Possible explanation: I used 3 as an addend

4 times to show that Ryan bought 4 packages with 3 juice boxes

in each.

Name _____

1. Derek has 12 sweaters. He places an equal number of sweaters into 2 drawers.

How many sweaters are in each drawer?

Ⓐ 2   Ⓒ **6**

Ⓑ 4   Ⓓ 8

2. Megan found 36 seashells. She put an equal number of shells in each of 4 piles. How many seashells are in each pile?

Ⓐ 32

Ⓑ **9**

Ⓒ 6

Ⓓ 4

3. Mr. Jackson has 16 flashcards. He gives an equal number of flashcards to 4 groups.

How many flashcards does Mr. Jackson give to each group?

Ⓐ **4**   Ⓒ 12

Ⓑ 8   Ⓓ 16

4. Linda picked 48 flowers. She placed them equally into 8 vases. How many flowers are in each vase?

Ⓐ 4   Ⓒ **6**

Ⓑ 5   Ⓓ 7

5. Nora says you cannot share 9 things in equal groups because 9 is an odd number. Do you agree or disagree? Explain.

Disagree; Possible explanation: Nora is right that 9 is an

odd number, but she could divide 9 things into 3 equal

groups of 3.

Name _____

1. Elle puts 24 charms into groups of 4. How many groups of charms are there?

Ⓐ 4

Ⓑ **6**

Ⓒ 20

Ⓓ 28

2. A sporting goods store has 72 baseball caps in stacks of 8 caps each. How many stacks of baseball caps are there?

Ⓐ 7

Ⓑ 8

Ⓒ **9**

Ⓓ 11

3. Heather places 32 stamps into groups of 8. How many groups of stamps are there?

Ⓐ 12

Ⓑ 8

Ⓒ 6

Ⓓ **4**

4. Mr. Smith wants to divide his students into groups of 6 for the planetarium tour. How many groups of 6 can be made with 18 students?

Ⓐ 2

Ⓑ **3**

Ⓒ 6

Ⓓ 9

5. Gary says that if you start with an even number of things to divide, you must have an even number of groups. Use an example to show that Gary's idea is wrong.
Possible example: start with 10 counters. You can divide

10 counters into 5 equal groups of 2. Since 5 is an odd

number, Gary is wrong. An even number can be divided

into an even or an odd number of groups.

Answer Key

1. The Bike Shack displays 45 bikes grouped by color. There are 5 bikes in each group. How many colors of bikes are on display?

☐ colors

5 [_____] 5

45 bikes

Ⓐ 5　　Ⓒ 8
Ⓑ 7　Ⓓ 9

2. Rico went for a 12 mile bike ride. He stopped every 3 miles to take pictures. How many times did Rico stop during his bike ride?

☐ times

3 [_____] 3

12 miles

Ⓐ 3　　Ⓒ 9
Ⓑ 4　Ⓓ 15

3. Amber divided her marbles evenly among 3 friends.

Which division equation is represented by the picture?

Ⓐ 3 ÷ 3 = 1

Ⓑ 18 ÷ 3 = 6

Ⓒ 18 ÷ 2 = 9

Ⓓ 21 ÷ 3 = 7

4. There are 16 students in the violin class. Mrs. Lau divides them into 4 equal groups. Explain how the model helps you find how many students are in each group. Write the division equation.

[☐ | ☐ | ☐ | ☐]

Possible explanation: 16 students
the model has 4 equal parts that represent the 4 groups of students.
The bracket shows there are 16 students in all. 16 ÷ 4 = 4.

---

1. Julio has a collection of coins. He puts the coins in 2 equal groups. There are 7 coins in each group.

0 1 2 3 4 5 6 7 8 9 10 11 12 13 14 15

How many coins does Julio have in all?

Ⓐ 7　Ⓑ 9　**Ⓒ 14**　Ⓓ 15

2. Mrs. Riley buys 3 packages of mangos to make a large fruit salad. Each package contains 2 mangos.

0 1 2 3 4 5 6 7 8 9 10

How many mangos does Mrs. Riley have in all?

Ⓐ 4　Ⓑ 5　**Ⓒ 6**　Ⓓ 8

3. Mr. Walters was cleaning his closet. He packed 2 shoes in each of 5 shoeboxes to donate to charity.

0 1 2 3 4 5 6 7 8 9 10

How many shoes did he pack in all?

Ⓐ 3　Ⓑ 7　Ⓒ 9　**Ⓓ 10**

4. Luis has 3 boxes of cars. There are 3 cars in each box.

0 1 2 3 4 5 6 7 8 9 10

How many cars does Luis have in all?

Ⓐ 10　Ⓑ 9　Ⓒ 8　Ⓓ 6

5. Rochelle makes 5 costumes using 3 yards of fabric for each. Describe how you would use a number line to find the total number of yards of fabric.

Possible answer: I would show 5 jumps of 3 units on
the number line. I would end on 15. So, Rochelle uses
15 yards of fabric.

---

1. Carson drew this array to show the number of pictures on one page of her photo album.

Which multiplication sentence does this array show?

Ⓐ 2 × 3 = 6　**Ⓒ 3 × 3 = 9**
Ⓑ 4 × 4 = 16　Ⓓ 3 × 2 = 6

2. Paco drew an array with 3 rows. Each row has 7 squares. Which multiplication sentence describes the array?

Ⓐ 2 × 8 = 16　**Ⓒ 3 × 7 = 21**
Ⓑ 2 × 9 = 18　Ⓓ 3 × 8 = 24

3. Rita arranged counters in 5 rows with 7 counters in each row. Which array shows how many counters she arranged in all?

Ⓐ

Ⓑ

Ⓒ

Ⓓ

4. Geoff stacked 16 cans of paint in 2 rows in his store. He put the same number of cans in each row. Draw an array to show his display.

How many cans of paint are in each row of the display?
8 cans

---

1. There are 4 tables in the school library. Four students are sitting at each table. Brett made this model with counters to show the total number of students sitting in the library. How many students are sitting in the library?

Ⓐ 8
Ⓑ 10
Ⓒ 12
Ⓓ 16

2. Lily goes on 6 rides at the carnival. The cost of each ride is $2. How much do the rides cost in all?

Ⓐ $14　　Ⓒ $10
Ⓑ $12　Ⓓ $8

3. Tara rode her bike to work 4 days this week. She rode a total of 9 miles each day. How many total miles did Tara ride her bike?

Ⓐ 13 miles　**Ⓒ 36 miles**
Ⓑ 18 miles　Ⓓ 45 miles

4. Max has 4 boxes of pencils. There are 6 pencils in each box. Max draws the model at right to show how many pencils he has in all. Write a multiplication sentence that the model can represent and tell how many pencils Max has in all. Explain how the model represents the sentence you wrote.

4 × 6 = 24. Max has 24 pencils in all. Each group
represents a box of pencils. Each dot inside a group
represents one of the 6 pencils in the box. There are 24
dots in all, which is the number of pencils that Max has.

Answer Key

Lesson 9
CC.3.OA.3

Name _____

1. Kyle bought 4 erasers at the school store. Each eraser cost 10¢.

| 10¢ | 10¢ | 10¢ | 10¢ |

_____ ¢

How much did the erasers cost in all?

Ⓐ 14¢ ● 40¢
Ⓑ 20¢ Ⓓ 44¢

2. Mrs. Howard's students stack their chairs at the end of the day. Each stack contains 5 chairs. If there are 6 stacks of chairs, how many chairs are stacked?

Ⓐ 15 Ⓒ 25
Ⓑ 20 ● 30

3. Aleesha has 10 packages of beads. There are 6 beads in each package. How many beads does Aleesha have altogether?

Ⓐ 16 ● 60
Ⓑ 30 Ⓓ 66

4. Tran buys an apple. He gives the store clerk 9 nickels. Each nickel has a value of 5 cents. How many cents does Tran give the store clerk?

● 45 cents
Ⓑ 35 cents
Ⓒ 14 cents
Ⓓ 10 cents

5. A gardener draws this picture to show how rose bushes will be planted in three flowerbeds. Each black dot represents one rose bush. How many rose bushes will there be in all? Explain how you used multiplication to find the total number of rose bushes.

There are 15 rose bushes in all. The model shows me that there are 3 groups of 5 rose bushes. When there are equal groups like this and you need to find how many in all, you can multiply. So, I multiplied 3 × 5 to find the total number of rose bushes.

Operations and Algebraic Thinking   9

Lesson 10
CC.3.OA.3

Name _____

1. Jason has 6 bookshelves in his room. There are 6 books on each shelf. How many books are there in all?

Ⓐ 12 Ⓒ 36
Ⓑ 24 Ⓓ 42

2. Madison makes 4 types of hair ribbons. She makes each type of ribbon using 3 different colors. How many hair ribbons does Madison make?

● 12
Ⓑ 10
Ⓒ 9
Ⓓ 7

3. Dora is making hexagons with straws. She uses 6 straws for each hexagon. If she makes 3 hexagons, how many straws does Dora use?

Ⓐ 9 Ⓒ 18
Ⓑ 12 ● 24

4. Elvira bought 4 packages of stickers. There are 6 stickers in each package. How many stickers did Elvira buy?

Ⓐ 12 Ⓒ 30
● 24 Ⓓ 36

5. Mr. Chung is a florist. He has to make 8 bunches of flowers. He needs 3 feet of ribbon to decorate each bunch. Make a model to help him find out how much ribbon he needs in all.

Write a multiplication sentence that the model represents and tell how many feet of ribbon Mr. Chung needs in all. Explain how you used the model to find the answer.

The model represents 8 × 3 = 24. So, Mr. Chung needs 24 feet of ribbon in all. I made 8 jumps of 3 equal spaces on the number line. The last number I landed on was 24.

10   Operations and Algebraic Thinking

Lesson 11
CC.3.OA.3

Name _____

1. During a field trip, 30 students in Mrs. Beckman's class were placed into groups of 6 students each for a tour of the museum. How many groups were there?

● 5 Ⓒ 7
Ⓑ 6 Ⓓ 8

2. Tao has 8 sand dollars in his collection. He makes a model to show how he shares his collection equally with his friend, Yom.

How many sand dollars does each boy get?

Ⓐ 2 Ⓒ 6
● 4 Ⓓ 8

3. Barry has 15 comic books. He wants to place his books in 3 equal piles. Which model shows how many comic books Barry should put in each pile?

Ⓐ

Ⓑ

●

Ⓓ

4. There are 54 party favors. Each of 6 tables will have the same number of party favors. How many party favors will go on each table? Explain how you can act out the problem with counters. **9 party favors; Possible explanation: I can draw 6 circles and put one counter in each circle until I use up all 54 counters. I find that each circle gets 9 counters so each table gets 9 favors.**

Operations and Algebraic Thinking   11

Lesson 12
CC.3.OA.3

Name _____

1. Mr. Burt shared 12 olives equally with each person in his family.

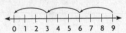

Which division equation is represented by the number line?

● 12 ÷ 3 = 4 Ⓒ 12 ÷ 2 = 6
Ⓑ 3 ÷ 3 = 1 Ⓓ 12 ÷ 6 = 2

2. Lionel bought a bag of favors for his party guests. He used repeated subtraction to help him divide the favors equally among his guests.

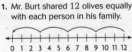

Which division equation matches the repeated subtraction?

Ⓐ 16 ÷ 2 = 8 Ⓒ 12 ÷ 3 = 4
Ⓑ 4 ÷ 4 = 1 ● 16 ÷ 4 = 4

3. Marco's mother bought 9 toy cars. She asked Marco to share the cars equally among his friends. Marco used a number line to help.

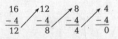

Which division equation is represented by the number line?

Ⓐ 3 ÷ 3 = 1 Ⓒ 9 ÷ 9 = 1
● 9 ÷ 3 = 3 Ⓓ 6 ÷ 3 = 2

4. Lola bought a bag of 15 apples for her friends. She used repeated subtraction to help her divide the apples equally among her friends.

$$\begin{array}{ccc} 15 & 10 & 5 \\ -5 & -5 & -5 \\ \hline 10 & 5 & 0 \end{array}$$

Which division equation matches the repeated subtraction?

Ⓐ 15 ÷ 15 = 1 ● 15 ÷ 5 = 3
Ⓑ 10 ÷ 5 = 2 Ⓓ 15 ÷ 1 = 15

5. How is repeated subtraction like counting back on a number line? Explain how both methods help you divide.
Possible explanation: they both start with the number you are dividing. Then they both subtract equal groups of the number you are dividing by. The number line shows the groups subtracted by counting back. The quotient is the number of jumps or the number of subtractions made.

12   Operations and Algebraic Thinking

© Houghton Mifflin Harcourt Publishing Company

108   **Answer Key**

1. Which division sentence best fits the array?

Ⓐ 16 ÷ 16 = 1

Ⓑ 16 ÷ 8 = 2

Ⓒ 16 ÷ 4 = 4

Ⓓ 16 ÷ 1 = 16

3. Which division sentence best fits the array?

Ⓐ 21 ÷ 1 = 21

Ⓑ 21 ÷ 3 = 7

Ⓒ 20 ÷ 5 = 4

Ⓓ 20 ÷ 10 = 2

2. Damian has 30 tiles. How many rows of 10 tiles can he make?

Ⓐ 27

Ⓑ 15

Ⓒ 10

Ⓓ 3

4. The 24 mailboxes in a building are in an array with 6 rows. How many mailboxes are in each row?

Ⓐ 4   Ⓒ 8

Ⓑ 6   Ⓓ 12

5. Write two division sentences for the array at the right. Explain how the array represents each sentence.

Possible answer: 12 ÷ 2 = 6; There are 12 squares

altogether and 2 squares in each row. So there are

6 rows. 12 ÷ 6 = 2; There are 12 squares altogether and

6 squares in each column. So, there are 2 columns.

---

1. Lionel has 14 mittens.

Which division equation is represented by the picture?

Ⓐ 7 ÷ 7 = 1

Ⓑ 2 ÷ 2 = 1

Ⓒ 14 ÷ 14 = 1

Ⓓ 14 ÷ 2 = 7

2. Garret practiced on the piano for the same amount of time each day for 2 days. He practiced a total of 4 hours. How many hours did Garret practice each day?

Ⓐ 1 hour   Ⓒ 6 hours

Ⓑ 2 hours   Ⓓ 8 hours

3. Ben needs 2 oranges to make a glass of orange juice. If oranges come in bags of 10, how many glasses of orange juice can he make using one bag of oranges?

Ⓐ 4   Ⓒ 6

Ⓑ 5   Ⓓ 8

4. Mrs. Conner has 16 shoes.

What division sentence is represented by the picture?

Ⓐ 80 ÷ 8 = 1

Ⓑ 16 ÷ 16 = 1

Ⓒ 16 ÷ 2 = 8

Ⓓ 2 ÷ 2 = 1

5. Hector read for the same amount of time each day for 2 days. He read for 6 hours in all. Explain how to find how many hours Hector read each day.

Possible answer: I drew 2 large circles for the 2 days

and drew a small circle in each of the large circles until

I had drawn 6 small circles. There were 3 small circles in

each of the large circles. So I could see that Hector read

for 3 hours each day.

---

1. The Bike Shack displays 45 bikes grouped by color. There are 5 bikes in each group. How many colors of bikes does the store have?

Ⓐ 7

Ⓑ 9

Ⓒ 20

Ⓓ 40

2. Mrs. Alvarez printed 35 pictures. She will group them into sets of 5. How many sets of pictures can she make?

Ⓐ 40   Ⓒ 7

Ⓑ 30   Ⓓ 6

3. Hannah made $40 selling hats. Each hat costs $5. She wants to know how many hats she sold. Hannah used a number line to help her.

0 5 10 15 20 25 30 35 40

Which division equation is represented by the number line?

Ⓐ 6 ÷ 6 = 1

Ⓑ 40 ÷ 10 = 4

Ⓒ 40 ÷ 4 = 10

Ⓓ 40 ÷ 5 = 8

4. Tara has 25 fresh muffins. She will freeze them in bags of 5 muffins. Explain how to use the number line to help show how many bags of muffins Tara can freeze.

0 5 10 15 20 25

Starting at 25, I drew jumps back by 5s: 25, 20, 15, 10,

5, 0. I made 5 jumps. So, Tara can freeze 5 bags of

5 muffins per bag.

---

1. The volleyball club plans to have 7 teams. There were 42 students who signed up to play. How many students will be on each team?

$7 \times \blacksquare = 42$

Ⓐ 5

Ⓑ 6

Ⓒ 7

Ⓓ 8

2. Duane needs 36 hats for a party. There are 6 hats in each package. How many packages of hats does Duane need to buy?

$p \times 6 = 36$

Ⓐ 2   Ⓒ 18

Ⓑ 6   Ⓓ 30

3. Pilar spent $48 on 6 books. The cost of each book was the same. Which equation can be used to find the cost of one book?

Ⓐ $48 × \blacksquare = 6$

Ⓑ $3 × \blacksquare = 6$

Ⓒ $48 × \blacksquare = 8$

Ⓓ $6 × \blacksquare = 48$

4. Mr. Perkins plans to teach 4 reading groups. If he has 28 students, how many students will be in each reading group?

$4 \times \blacksquare = 28$

Ⓐ 24   Ⓒ 7

Ⓑ 8   Ⓓ 6

5. Emily plans to buy 54 muffins for a breakfast party. There are 6 muffins in each package. How many packages will Emily need? Write an equation using the letter p to stand for the unknown factor. Explain how to find the unknown factor.

9 packages; $p \times 6 = 54$; Possible explanation: I can draw

an array with 54 tiles with 6 tiles in each row. There are

9 rows, so $p = 9$.

© Houghton Mifflin Harcourt Publishing Company

Answer Key

109

CC.3.OA.4

Name _____

1. Brian is dividing 64 baseball cards equally among 8 friends. How many baseball cards will each friend get?

Ⓐ 7
Ⓑ 8
Ⓒ 9
Ⓓ 10

2. Adam and his friends raked enough leaves to fill 48 bags. Each person filled 8 bags. How many people raked leaves?

Ⓐ 6
Ⓑ 5
Ⓒ 4
Ⓓ 3

3. Students celebrated Earth Day by planting 24 seedlings at 8 different locations in town. They planted the same number of seedlings at each location. How many seedlings did they plant at each location?

Ⓐ 6   Ⓒ 4
Ⓑ 5   **Ⓓ 3**

4. Keith arranged 40 toy cars in 8 equal rows. How many toy cars are in each row?

Ⓐ 4
Ⓑ 5
Ⓒ 6
Ⓓ 32

5. Eight friends planted 72 tulip bulbs. Each friend planted the same number of bulbs. Explain how to find the number of bulbs each friend planted.

Possible explanation: 72 bulbs are planted by 8 people.
Each person plants the same number of bulbs, so
divide. I can multiply to solve: eight times what number
is 72? 8 × 9 = 72, so 72 ÷ 8 = 9. So, each friend
planted 9 bulbs.

Operations and Algebraic Thinking   17

CC.3.OA.5

Name _____

1. Donna wrote 5 × 9 = 45. Which is a related number sentence?

Ⓐ 5 + 4 = 9   Ⓒ 5 × 5 = 25
Ⓑ 9 × 5 = 45   Ⓓ 4 × 5 = 20

2. Matthew made arrays with counters to show the Commutative Property of Multiplication.

Which multiplication sentences are shown by his arrays?

Ⓐ 3 × 4 = 12 and 4 × 3 = 12
Ⓑ 6 × 4 = 24 and 4 × 6 = 24
Ⓒ 6 × 2 = 12 and 2 × 6 = 12
Ⓓ 2 × 7 = 14 and 7 × 2 = 14

3. Greta put 6 coins into each of 3 stacks. She wrote 3 × 6 = 18. Which is a related number sentence?

Ⓐ 6 × 3 = 18
Ⓑ 6 + 3 = 9
Ⓒ 3 + 3 + 3 = 9
Ⓓ 6 × 6 = 36

4. Ben put 10 color pencils into each of 6 bags. He wrote 6 × 10 = 60 to represent the total. Which is a related multiplication sentence?

Ⓐ 10 × 10 = 100
Ⓑ 5 × 12 = 60
Ⓒ 6 × 6 = 36
Ⓓ 10 × 6 = 60

5. Write a multiplication sentence for the array. Then draw a different array you could make using the same two factors. Write the multiplication sentence for the array you drew.

2 × 4 = 8; 4 × 2 = 8.

18   Operations and Algebraic Thinking

CC.3.OA.5

Name _____

1. Sierra looked in 4 jars for marbles. In each jar she found 0 marbles. Which number sentence represents the total number of marbles Sierra found?

Ⓐ 4 + 0 = 4
Ⓑ 4 × 0 = 0
Ⓒ 4 × 1 = 4
Ⓓ 4 − 4 = 0

2. Robin found 1 pinecone under each of 3 trees. Which number sentence shows how many pinecones Robin found?

Ⓐ 3 − 3 = 0
Ⓑ 3 + 0 = 3
Ⓒ 3 × 0 = 0
Ⓓ 3 × 1 = 3

3. Juan bought a golf ball display case with 10 shelves. There are 0 golf balls on each shelf. Which number sentence shows how many golf balls Juan has in the display case now?

Ⓐ 10 − 0 = 10
Ⓑ 1 × 10 = 10
Ⓒ 10 × 0 = 0
Ⓓ 10 + 0 = 10

4. Aiden saw 4 lifeguard towers at the beach. Each tower had 1 lifeguard. Which number sentence represents the total number of lifeguards Aiden saw?

Ⓐ 4 × 4 = 16
Ⓑ 4 × 1 = 4
Ⓒ 1 × 1 = 1
Ⓓ 4 + 1 = 5

5. Franco says that when he multiplies any number by a factor, the product is always equal to the number. What is the factor? Explain how you know this is true.

The factor is 1; Possible explanation: the Identity
Property of Multiplication states that the product of any
number and 1 is that number. For example, 5 × 1 = 5
and 1 × 8 = 8.

Operations and Algebraic Thinking   19

CC.3.OA.5

Name _____

1. Henry and 5 friends are going to the movies. Tickets cost $8 each. Henry used this model to help him find the total cost of tickets.

Which shows one way to break apart the array to find the product?

Ⓐ (6 × 5) + (6 × 3)
Ⓑ (3 × 8) + (6 × 8)
Ⓒ (6 × 6) + (6 × 4)
Ⓓ 6 + (4 × 4)

2. Which number sentence is an example of the Distributive Property of Multiplication?

Ⓐ 7 × 8 = 50 + 6
Ⓑ 7 × 8 = 7 × (2 × 4)
Ⓒ 7 × 8 = 8 × 7
Ⓓ 7 × 8 = (7 × 4) + (7 × 4)

3. Which is equal to 7 × 9?

Ⓐ (7 × 3) + (7 × 3)
Ⓑ (7 × 3) × (7 × 3)
Ⓒ (7 × 3) + (7 × 6)
Ⓓ (7 × 3) × (7 × 6)

4. The array at right represents the product 4 × 9. Break apart the array to make two smaller arrays and write a multiplication sentence for each of them. Explain how to use the two smaller arrays to find 4 × 9.

Possible answer: the two smaller arrays show
4 × 5 = 20 and 4 × 4 = 16. The two smaller arrays
make up the big array. This means that the number of
squares in the big array is 20 + 16 = 36. So, 4 × 9 = 36.

20   Operations and Algebraic Thinking

Answer Key

Lesson 21
CC.3.OA.5

1. Which number sentence is an example of the Associative Property of Multiplication?

　Ⓐ $4 \times 2 = 2 \times 4$

　Ⓑ $(4 \times 2) \times 2 = 4 \times (2 \times 2)$

　Ⓒ $4 \times 2 = (4 \times 1) + (4 \times 1)$

　Ⓓ $4 \times (2 + 2) = (4 \times 2) + (4 \times 2)$

2. Which is equal to $(2 \times 2) \times 5$?

　Ⓐ $2 \times (2 + 5)$

　Ⓑ $2 \times (2 \times 5)$

　Ⓒ $(2 \times 2) \times (2 \times 5)$

　Ⓓ $(2 + 5) \times (2 + 5)$

3. Corey has 3 stacks of boxes. In each stack are 3 boxes with 2 trains in each box. How many trains does he have in all?

　Ⓐ 6　　　　Ⓒ 18

　Ⓑ 9　　　　Ⓓ 27

4. There are 2 walls in Yolanda's classroom that each have 2 rows of pictures. Each row has 3 pictures. How many pictures are on these walls in Yolanda's classroom?

　Ⓐ 12　　　Ⓒ 6

　Ⓑ 7　　　　Ⓓ 4

5. Marshall has 3 bags in each of his 2 toy chests. Each bag has 5 marbles. To find how many marbles there are in all, Marshall writes $(3 \times 2) \times 5$ and $3 \times (2 \times 5)$. Which way can be used to find how many marbles there are in all? Explain your answer.

Possible answer: both ways can be used to find the

correct answer. In $(3 \times 2) \times 5$, you multiply (3×2) first.

In $3 \times (2 \times 5)$, you multiply (2×5) first.

So $(3 \times 2) \times 5 = 6 \times 5$, and $6 \times 5 = 30$; $3 \times (2 \times 5) =$

3×10, and $3 \times 10 = 30$. So, both ways can be used to

find that there are 30 marbles in all.

Lesson 22
CC.3.OA.5

1. There are 0 books and 4 bookshelves. How many books are on each bookshelf?

　Ⓐ 0　　　　Ⓒ 3

　Ⓑ 1　　　　Ⓓ 4

2. Percy paid $9 for some notebooks for school. Each notebook cost $1. How many notebooks did Percy buy?

　Ⓐ 0

　Ⓑ 1

　Ⓒ 8

　Ⓓ 9

3. Otis paid $7 for some markers for school. Each marker cost $1. How many markers did Otis buy?

　Ⓐ 0

　Ⓑ 1

　Ⓒ 6

　Ⓓ 7

4. Norma made 8 cat treats. She gave an equal number of cat treats to each of 8 cats. How many cat treats did Norma give to each cat?

　Ⓐ 0

　Ⓑ 1

　Ⓒ 4

　Ⓓ 8

5. Karen has 5 flower pots and 0 flowers. How many flowers are in each flower pot? Explain. Then write the division sentence.

0 flowers; Possible explanation: if there are no flowers,

there is nothing to place in a group. Each group has

0 flowers. So $0 \div 5 = 0$.

Lesson 23
CC.3.OA.6

1. Cindy made 24 bracelets using 8 different colors. She made the same number of bracelets of each color. How many bracelets of each color did she make?

　$8 \times \blacksquare = 24$　　$24 \div 8 = \blacksquare$

　Ⓐ 2　　　　Ⓒ 4

　Ⓑ 3　　　　Ⓓ 8

2. There are 32 chairs in Mr. Owen's art room. There are 4 chairs at each table. Which equation can be used to find the number of tables in the art room?

　Ⓐ $4 + \blacksquare = 32$

　Ⓑ $32 + 4 = \blacksquare$

　Ⓒ $4 \times 32 = \blacksquare$

　Ⓓ $\blacksquare \times 4 = 32$

3. Yolanda knitted 15 scarves in 3 different colors. She knitted the same number of scarves of each color. How many scarves of each color did she make?

　$3 \times \blacksquare = 15$　　$15 \div 3 = \blacksquare$

　Ⓐ 5　　　　Ⓒ 9

　Ⓑ 8　　　　Ⓓ 12

4. Mike wrote these related equations. Which number completes both equations?

　$6 \times \blacksquare = 48$　　$48 \div 6 = \blacksquare$

　Ⓐ 9　　　　Ⓒ 7

　Ⓑ 8　　　　Ⓓ 6

5. Write a multiplication equation and a division equation for the array. Explain why those two operations make sense when describing the same array.

$3 \times 9 = 27$ and $27 \div 3 = 9$; Possible explanation: the

array shows 3 rows of 9 dots, which is $3 \times 9 = 27$ dots

in all. You can also look at the array as 27 dots divided

equally into 3 rows, which is represented by $27 \div 3 = 9$

dots in each row.

Lesson 24
CC.3.OA.7

1. There are 7 apartments on every floor of Sean's apartment building. The building has 5 floors. How many apartments are in Sean's apartment building?

　Ⓐ 12

　Ⓑ 21

　Ⓒ 35

　Ⓓ 42

2. Sandy made greeting cards for a craft show. She put 7 greeting cards in each of 7 boxes. How many greeting cards did Sandy make altogether?

　Ⓐ 56

　Ⓑ 49

　Ⓒ 28

　Ⓓ 14

3. Mike sent 7 postcards to each of 4 friends when he was on vacation. How many postcards did Mike send altogether?

　Ⓐ 11

　Ⓑ 14

　Ⓒ 21

　Ⓓ 28

4. There are 9 vans taking students to the museum. Each van is carrying 7 students. How many students are in the vans?

　Ⓐ 16

　Ⓑ 63

　Ⓒ 70

　Ⓓ 77

5. The students in Ms. Guzman's class picked 6 baskets of peaches. They put 7 peaches in each basket. Write a multiplication sentence to show how many peaches the students picked in all. Explain why a multiplication sentence can be used to represent the total.

$6 \times 7 = 42$. The problem says that the same number of peaches is in

each basket. You can multiply when you have equal groups and you

want to find how many in all.

Answer Key

1. Ashley buys 8 fishbowls. There are 2 goldfish in each bowl. How many goldfish did Ashley buy?

   Ⓐ 4
   Ⓑ 8
   Ⓒ 16
   Ⓓ 24

2. There are 8 teams setting up booths for the school fair. There are 7 people on each team. How many people are setting up booths?

   Ⓐ 28   Ⓒ 56
   Ⓑ 48   Ⓓ 64

3. Students' exhibits at a science fair are judged in 5 categories. Akio's exhibit received 8 points in each category. How many total points did Akio's exhibit receive?

   Ⓐ 20
   Ⓑ 40
   Ⓒ 48
   Ⓓ 56

4. Liz buys 6 flowerpots. There are 8 flowers in each pot. How many flowers did Liz buy?

   Ⓐ 4   Ⓒ 40
   Ⓑ 14   Ⓓ 48

5. There are 8 groups of dogs in a dog show. There are 8 dogs in each group. Jake draws the model at right to show all the dogs in the show. Explain how Jake can use the model and multiplication to find how many dogs there are in all without counting every square in the model.

   Possible answer: the model shows 8 rows of 8. Jake can multiply 8 × 8 to find how many squares there are without counting them all. 8 × 8 = 64. So, Jake can say there are 64 dogs in all.

---

1. Mika bought 3 boxes of bouncy balls. Each box contains 9 bouncy balls. How many bouncy balls did Mika buy in all?

   Ⓐ 12
   Ⓑ 18
   Ⓒ 24
   Ⓓ 27

2. There are 8 students in the camera club. Each student took 9 pictures. How many pictures did the students take altogether?

   Ⓐ 81
   Ⓑ 72
   Ⓒ 64
   Ⓓ 17

3. Shana bought 5 bags of hard pretzels. Each bag contains 9 pretzels. How many hard pretzels did Shana buy in all?

   Ⓐ 14
   Ⓑ 40
   Ⓒ 45
   Ⓓ 50

4. Raul has 6 shoeboxes on his bookshelf. If he has 9 toy robots in each shoebox, how many toy robots does Raul have?

   Ⓐ 63
   Ⓑ 54
   Ⓒ 36
   Ⓓ 15

5. Maria wrote 4 pages in her journal each day for 9 days. How many pages did Maria write in all? Explain how you know.

   Maria wrote 36 pages in all. I know because reading 4 pages each day for 9 days is like 9 groups of 4 things. You multiply when you have equal groups and you want to find how many in all. When I multiply 9 × 4, the product is 36.

---

1. Han wrote a set of related facts for the array below. Which equation is **not** related to this array?

   Ⓐ 3 × 4 = 12
   Ⓑ 6 × 2 = 12
   Ⓒ 12 ÷ 4 = 3
   Ⓓ 12 ÷ 3 = 4

2. Lucy writes a set of related facts. One of the facts she writes is 24 ÷ 6 = 4. Which equation is related to this fact?

   Ⓐ 8 × 3 = 24
   Ⓑ 24 ÷ 8 = 3
   Ⓒ 6 × 4 = 24
   Ⓓ 24 ÷ 3 = 8

3. Fritz wrote a set of related facts for the array below. Which equation is **not** related to this array?

   Ⓐ 6 × 3 = 18
   Ⓑ 6 ÷ 2 = 3
   Ⓒ 3 × 2 = 6
   Ⓓ 2 × 3 = 6

4. Alex uses the numbers 3, 4, and 12 to write multiplication and division related facts. Which equation is one of the related facts that Alex writes?

   Ⓐ 3 + 4 = 7
   Ⓑ 12 − 8 = 4
   Ⓒ 12 ÷ 6 = 2
   Ⓓ 4 × 3 = 12

5. Peter writes a set of related facts. One of the facts he writes is 18 ÷ 6 = 3. Write a division equation that is related to that fact. Explain how an array helps you.

   18 ÷ 3 = 6; Possible explanation: I can make an array of 18 counters with 6 counters in each row to show Peter's equation. There will be 3 equal rows. The array also shows 18 counters divided into 6 equal groups with 3 in each group or 18 ÷ 3 = 6.

---

1. Larah found 50 pinecones. She put 10 pinecones in each bag. How many bags did Larah use?

   Ⓐ 5
   Ⓑ 6
   Ⓒ 9
   Ⓓ 10

2. Michael wants to display his model car collection on shelves. He has 60 model cars. He puts 10 cars on each shelf. How many shelves does Michael use?

   Ⓐ 6
   Ⓑ 8
   Ⓒ 10
   Ⓓ 70

3. There are 20 students in science class. There are 10 students sitting at each table. Which division sentence shows how many tables have students at them?

   Ⓐ 20 ÷ 4 = 5
   Ⓑ 20 ÷ 10 = 2
   Ⓒ 10 ÷ 5 = 2
   Ⓓ 10 ÷ 10 = 1

4. Stickers cost 10¢ each. How many stickers can Todd buy with 80¢?

   Ⓐ 10
   Ⓑ 9
   Ⓒ 8
   Ⓓ 7

5. Vonda says, "I like to divide by 10. The quotient is right there!" Tell what Vonda means by explaining how to solve 90 ÷ 10.

   Possible answer: Vonda means that dividing by 10 is like dividing by 1 because the quotient is the number in the tens place of the number being divided. In 90 ÷ 10, 9 is in the tens place; the quotient is 9.

Lesson 29
CC.3.OA.7

1. Steve and his family traveled 12 miles on a sunset cruise. Every 3 miles, the boat stopped for people to take pictures. How many times did the boat stop for pictures?

Ⓐ 4
Ⓑ 6
Ⓒ 9
Ⓓ 15

2. Martina plays tennis. She gets 21 new tennis balls. They come in cans of 3. How many cans of tennis balls did Martina get?

Ⓐ 18
Ⓑ 8
Ⓒ 7
Ⓓ 6

3. Jake walked 15 miles in a walk-a-thon. Every 3 miles, he stopped for a rest. How many times did Jake stop for a rest?

Ⓐ 4
Ⓑ 5
Ⓒ 6
Ⓓ 12

4. There are 27 students in Mr. Garcia's class. The class is going on a field trip to a water park. Mr. Garcia separates the students into groups of 3. How many groups will Mr. Garcia make?

Ⓐ 30
Ⓑ 24
Ⓒ 14
Ⓓ 9

5. Zelda is teaching her sister about division. Explain how Zelda can use a picture to show how to divide 18 cubes into 3 equal groups.

Possible answer: I can draw a picture that shows 3 circles. Then I

can draw an X in each circle until I have drawn 18 Xs. Each circle will

have 6 Xs in it. So 18 ÷ 3 = 6.

Operations and Algebraic Thinking   29

Lesson 30
CC.3.OA.7

1. Ellen is making 4 gift baskets for her friends. She has 16 prizes she wants to divide equally among the baskets. How many prizes should she put in each basket?

Ⓐ 4
Ⓑ 8
Ⓒ 12
Ⓓ 20

2. Casey has 20 coins. She places them in equal stacks. There are 4 coins in each stack. How many stacks of coins are there?

Ⓐ 5
Ⓑ 6
Ⓒ 7
Ⓓ 8

3. Jim collected 28 seashells at the beach. He arranged them in equal rows. There are 4 seashells in each row. How many rows of seashells are there?

Ⓐ 6
Ⓑ 7
Ⓒ 24
Ⓓ 30

4. Holly is making 4 veggie trays for a party. She wants to divide 36 carrot sticks equally among the trays. How many carrot sticks will she put on each tray?

Ⓐ 7
Ⓑ 8
Ⓒ 9
Ⓓ 32

5. Mrs. Sosa bought a stuffed toy for each of her 4 grandchildren. She spent $24. Each toy cost the same amount. Explain how to find the cost of each stuffed toy.

Possible explanation: I have to divide because I know the total

cost ($24) and how many toys (4) Mrs. Sosa got with that money.

I will divide $24 ÷ 4 to find the cost of each toy. $24 ÷ 4 = $6.

30   Operations and Algebraic Thinking

Lesson 31
CC.3.OA.7

1. Pedro uses 30 game pieces to play a game. He gives 6 players the same number of game pieces. How many game pieces does each player get?

Ⓐ 4   Ⓒ 10
Ⓑ 5   Ⓓ 15

2. Each team at a hockey tournament has 6 players. How many teams are there if 42 players are at the tournament?

Ⓐ 5
Ⓑ 6
Ⓒ 7
Ⓓ 8

3. There are picnic tables at the park. Each picnic table seats 6 people. How many picnic tables are needed to seat 24 people?

Ⓐ 3
Ⓑ 4
Ⓒ 5
Ⓓ 6

4. Luis uses 36 marbles to play a game There are 6 players in the game. If each player gets the same number of marbles, how many marbles does each player get?

Ⓐ 30   Ⓒ 12
Ⓑ 18   Ⓓ 6

5. The same number goes in the box in both equations. Explain how to find the unknown factor and quotient using what you know about multiplication and division.

$6 \times \blacksquare = 54$ $54 \div 6 = \blacksquare$

Possible explanation: I needed to know what number times

6 is 54. I know that 6 × 10 = 60, so I tried 6 × 9, and that

is 54. Then I tried 9 in the division equation, and it works

there, too. Six 9s are 54, so 54 divided by 6 is also 9.

Operations and Algebraic Thinking   31

Lesson 32
CC.3.OA.7

1. Ming divided 35 marbles among 7 different friends. Each friend received the same number of marbles. How many marbles did Ming give to each friend?

$35 \div 7 = a$
$7 \times a = 35$

Ⓐ 4   Ⓒ 6
Ⓑ 5   Ⓓ 7

2. Ana used 49 strawberries to make 7 strawberry milkshakes. She used the same number of strawberries in each milkshake. How many strawberries did Ana use in each milkshake?

Ⓐ 4   Ⓒ 6
Ⓑ 5   Ⓓ 7

3. Joni texted her dad every day for 42 days. How many weeks did Joni text her dad? [Hint: 1 week has 7 days.]

Ⓐ 5 weeks   Ⓒ 7 weeks
Ⓑ 6 weeks   Ⓓ 8 weeks

4. Shang divided 28 postcards among 7 different people. Each person received the same number of postcards. How many postcards did Shang give to each person?

$28 \div 7 = n$
$7 \times n = 28$

Ⓐ 4   Ⓒ 6
Ⓑ 5   Ⓓ 21

5. The calendar shows the dates in May. Explain how to use the calendar to help find 28 divided by 7.

			May 2011			
Sun	Mon	Tue	Wed	Thu	Fri	Sat
1	2	3	4	5	6	7
8	9	10	11	12	13	14
15	16	17	18	19	20	21
22	23	24	25	26	27	28
29	30	31				

Possible explanation: the 7 days in a week are

like equal groups of 7. The calendar is like an

array with 4 full rows. I find 28 on the calendar

and see how many weeks it takes to get to 28.

It takes 4 weeks; 4 × 7 = 28, and 28 ÷ 7 = 4.

32   Operations and Algebraic Thinking

Answer Key   **113**

1. Mrs. Torres separates 45 students into 9 equal groups for a field trip. How many students are in each group?

Ⓐ 4   Ⓒ 6
● 5   Ⓓ 7

2. Carla sells homemade pretzels in bags with 9 pretzels in each bag. She sells 54 pretzels in all. How many bags of pretzels does she sell?

● 6   Ⓒ 4
Ⓑ 5   Ⓓ 3

3. A flower shop sells tulips in bunches of 9. It sells 27 tulips. How many bunches of tulips does the shop sell?

Ⓐ 2   Ⓒ 4
● 3   Ⓓ 9

4. There are 36 athletes at a baseball workshop. A baseball team has 9 players. How many teams can be formed?

Ⓐ 7   Ⓒ 5
Ⓑ 6   ● 4

5. Andy keeps mixing up 9×9 and 9×2. This makes it harder to learn $81 \div 9$ and $18 \div 9$. Explain how these multiplication and division facts are alike and how they are different.

Possible answer: 9×9 and 9×2 are alike because they both can be thought of as 9 groups. 9×9 is 9 groups of 9, and 9×2 is 9 groups of 2. The number of things in the groups is different. $81 \div 9$ and $18 \div 9$ are alike because they can be shown by 9 groups or groups of 9. They are different because 81 is greater than 18 so there will not be as many things in each group if the number of groups is the same.

1. During the first week of school, 345 students bought their lunch. During the second week of school, 23 fewer students bought their lunch than the week before. How many students bought their lunch in those two weeks?

Ⓐ 322   Ⓒ 667
Ⓑ 368   Ⓓ 713

2. On Monday, 117 students signed up to plant trees in the park. On Tuesday, 16 fewer students signed up than on Monday. How many students signed up to plant trees on Monday and Tuesday?

● 218   Ⓒ 118
Ⓑ 158   Ⓓ 101

3. In one week, 103 students were absent. The next week, 17 fewer students were absent than the week before. How many students were absent in those two weeks?

Ⓐ 86   ● 189
Ⓑ 120   Ⓓ 223

4. For two days, Imani counted taxis that passed her house from 4:30 to 4:45 P.M. She counted 33 taxis on Monday. That was 19 fewer than the number of taxis she counted on Tuesday. How many taxis did Imani count on both days?

Ⓐ 14   Ⓒ 52
Ⓑ 33   ● 85

5. Draw bar models to solve $45 + 92 = \blacksquare$ and $92 - \blacksquare = 45$. Explain how the models are alike and how they are different.

Check students' drawings.

Possible explanation: for the addition problem, you know the 2 smaller parts and find the whole. In the subtraction problem, you know the whole and one part. You need to find the other part.

1. Edith sorts buttons into 4 groups. Each group contains 3 buttons. How many buttons does Edith sort?

buttons

Ⓐ 4   ● 12
Ⓑ 11   Ⓓ 16

2. Hector has 4 groups of blocks with 2 blocks in each group. He uses 3 of the blocks for a project. How many blocks does Hector have left?

Ⓐ 3   Ⓒ 9
● 5   Ⓓ 11

3. John sold 3 baskets of peaches at the market. Each basket contained 6 peaches. How many peaches did John sell?

peaches

Ⓐ 36   ● 18
Ⓑ 30   Ⓓ 9

4. Sophia buys 3 baskets of apples to make applesauce. Each basket has 9 apples in it. How many apples does Sophia buy in all?

● 27   Ⓒ 18
Ⓑ 24   Ⓓ 9

5. Landon sorted his trading cards into 3 groups. Each group had 7 cards. How many trading cards does he have in all? Use the bar model to solve. Explain your answer.

7	7	7

21 trading cards

Possible answer: I wrote 7 in each box to show the 7 cards in each group. I multiplied to solve: $3 \times 7 = 21$.

1. Bella is planning to write in her journal. Some pages will have two journal entries on them, and other pages will have three journal entries on them. If Bella wants to make 18 entries, how many different ways can she write them in her journal?

● 2   Ⓒ 5
Ⓑ 4   Ⓓ 10

2. Jayme wants to make $1.50 using dollars, half dollars, and quarters. How many different ways can she make $1.50?

Ⓐ 4   ● 6
Ⓑ 5   Ⓓ 7

3. Toddrick has a photo album. Some pages have one photo on them, and other pages have two photos on them. If Toddrick has 9 photos, how many different ways can he put them in the album?

Ⓐ 2   ● 4
Ⓑ 3   Ⓓ 5

4. Myra has 30 cousins. Each month for the past 5 months, she has seen 2 different cousins. How many more cousins does she have to see before she has seen all 30 cousins?

Ⓐ 18   Ⓒ 25
● 20   Ⓓ 28

5. Erin wants to arrange flower bouquets in rows for a reception. Each row can have 4 or 6 bouquets. She has a total of 22 bouquets and wants to know how many different ways she can arrange them. Explain how Erin could make a table to find how many different ways she can arrange the bouquets.

Erin can make a table with three rows. The top row of the table would show rows with 4 bouquets. The second row of the table would show rows with 6 bouquets. The bottom row of the table would show the total number of bouquets, which is 22. She could fill in the different combinations of numbers for 4 or 6 bouquets in the table to find all the different ways.

Answer Key

Lesson 37
CC.3.OA.8

1. Gary bought 4 packs of cards. Each pack had the same number of cards. A friend gave him 3 more cards. Now he has 35 cards in all. How many cards were in each pack?

Ⓐ 42   Ⓒ 8

Ⓑ 28   Ⓓ 7

2. Mrs. Jackson bought 5 packages of juice boxes. Each package had the same number of juice boxes. She opened one package and gave 3 juice boxes away. Now she has 27 juice boxes. How many juice boxes were in each package?

Ⓐ 6   Ⓒ 24

Ⓑ 8   Ⓓ 35

3. Ms. King bought 7 packages of raisin boxes. Each package had the same number of raisin boxes. She opened one package and gave 5 raisin boxes away. Now she has 51 raisin boxes. How many raisin boxes were in each package?

Ⓐ 56   Ⓒ 8

Ⓑ 12   Ⓓ 7

4. George had 6 sheets of animal stickers. Each sheet had the same number of stickers. A friend gave him 4 more animal stickers. Now he has 40 animal stickers. How many animal stickers were on each sheet?

Ⓐ 50   Ⓒ 10

Ⓑ 24   Ⓓ 6

5. Ruby saved $12 to buy cat toys. Her uncle gives her $3 more. Each cat toy costs $5. Explain the steps needed to find how many cat toys Ruby can buy.

Possible answer: first, add the money Ruby saved ($12) to the $3 her uncle gave her. She has $15. Then, divide to see how many $5 toys Ruby can buy with $15. Since $3 \times \$5 = \$15$, I know that $15 can buy 3 $5 cat toys.

Operations and Algebraic Thinking   37

Lesson 38
CC.3.OA.8

1. Amber uses the order of operations to solve the equation below.

$$63 - 49 \div 7 = b$$

What is the unknown number?

Ⓐ $b = 2$ Ⓒ $b = 55$

Ⓑ $b = 14$ Ⓓ $b = 56$

2. Aki uses the order of operations to solve the equation below.

$$3 + 12 \div 3 = c$$

What is the unknown number?

Ⓐ $c = 7$ Ⓒ $c = 5$

Ⓑ $c = 6$ Ⓓ $c = 4$

3. Kayla uses the order of operations to solve the equation below.

$$78 - 54 \div 6 = h$$

What is the unknown number?

Ⓐ $h = 4$ Ⓒ $h = 69$

Ⓑ $h = 24$ Ⓓ $h = 70$

4. Deon uses the order of operations to solve the equation below.

$$3 + 7 \times 3 = x$$

What is the unknown number?

Ⓐ $x = 13$ Ⓒ $x = 24$

Ⓑ $x = 21$ Ⓓ $x = 30$

5. Zeke and Luz both found the value of m in this equation:

$$16 - 7 \times 2 = m$$

Zeke says $m = 18$. Luz says $m = 2$. Who is right? Explain your reason.

Possible answer: Luz is right because she followed the order of operations. She multiplied 7×2 and then subtracted 14 from 16. Zeke solved from left to right, but he subtracted before he multiplied. He found $16 - 7 = 9$, and then $9 \times 2 = 18$.

38

Operations and Algebraic Thinking

Lesson 39
CC.3.OA.9

1. Kara wrote this number sentence to show how many yellow stickers and green stickers she earned. Which describes Kara's number sentence?

$$7 + 0 = 7$$

Ⓐ Commutative Property of Addition

Ⓑ Identity Property of Addition

Ⓒ odd + odd = odd

Ⓓ even + even = even

2. Pablo finds the sum of two addends. The sum is odd. Which statement is **true** about the addends?

Ⓐ Both addends are odd.

Ⓑ Both addends are even.

Ⓒ The addends are both odd or both even.

Ⓓ One addend is odd and one addend is even.

3. Maria wrote the number sentence $4 + 7 = 11$. Which number sentence shows the Commutative Property of Addition?

Ⓐ $11 - 4 = 7$

Ⓑ $3 + 4 = 7$

Ⓒ $4 + 7 = 11$

Ⓓ $7 + 4 = 11$

4. Gregory finds the sum of two addends. The sum is even. Which could **not** be Gregory's addends?

Ⓐ $3 + 10$

Ⓑ $7 + 1$

Ⓒ $7 + 7$

Ⓓ $10 + 12$

5. Ruby says she has read an even number of books. She has read 9 fiction books and 8 nonfiction books. Is Ruby correct? Explain your answer.

No. Possible explanation: Ruby has read an odd number of books because $9 + 8 = 17$, and 17 is an odd number.

Operations and Algebraic Thinking   39

Lesson 40
CC.3.OA.9

Use the multiplication table for 1–4.

×	0	1	2	3	4	5	6	7	8	9	10
0	0	0	0	0	0	0	0	0	0	0	0
1	0	1	2	3	4	5	6	7	8	9	10
2	0	2	4	6	8	10	12	14	16	18	20
3	0	3	6	9	12	15	18	21	24	27	30
4	0	4	8	12	16	20	24	28	32	36	40
5	0	5	10	15	20	25	30	35	40	45	50
6	0	6	12	18	24	30	36	42	48	54	60
7	0	7	14	21	28	35	42	49	56	63	70
8	0	8	16	24	32	80	48	56	64	72	80
9	0	9	18	27	36	45	54	63	72	81	90
10	0	10	20	30	40	50	60	70	80	90	100

1. Which row of the table has only even numbers?

Ⓐ the row for 3

Ⓑ the row for 4

Ⓒ the row for 7

Ⓓ the row for 9

2. Which describes a pattern in the column for 5?

Ⓐ All the products are even.

Ⓑ All the products are odd.

Ⓒ Each product is twice the product above it.

Ⓓ Each product is 5 more than the product above it.

3. Which product is even?

Ⓐ 3×7

Ⓑ 4×5

Ⓒ 5×3

Ⓓ 9×1

4. Describe as many patterns as you can in the row for 9.

Possible answers: the products repeat–odd, even. Each product is 9 more than the product to its left. Starting in the second column, each ones digit is 1 less than the ones digit to the left, and each tens digit is 1 more than the tens digit to the left.

40

Operations and Algebraic Thinking

Answer Key

115

Lesson 41
CC.3.OA.9

1. Lori is making bracelets. The table shows how many beads she will need. Which two numbers come next?

Bracelets	2	3	4	5	6
Beads	10	15	20	▪	▪

  Ⓐ 25 and 30   Ⓒ 30 and 35
  Ⓑ 25 and 35   Ⓓ 30 and 40

2. Sofia is making omelets. The table shows how many eggs she will need. Which of the following describes a pattern in this table?

Omelets	2	3	4	5	6
Eggs	6	9	12	15	18

  Ⓐ Add 4.   Ⓒ Multiply by 3.
  Ⓑ Subtract 3. Ⓓ Multiply by 4.

5. One vase holds 5 roses. Complete the table to find the number of roses in 7 vases. Write the number of roses in 7 vases.

Vases	1	2	3	4	5	6	7
Roses	5	10	15	**20**	**25**	**30**	**35**

  35 roses

3. Stephanie and John made a table about spiders. Which of the following describes a pattern in this table?

Spiders	2	3	4	5	6
Legs	16	24	32	40	48

  Ⓐ Add 14.   Ⓒ Multiply by 6.
  Ⓑ Subtract 35. Ⓓ Multiply by 8.

4. Bobby made a table about ants. Which number completes the pattern in this table?

Ants	3	4	5	6	7
Legs	18	24	30	▪	42

  Ⓐ 6   Ⓒ 36
  Ⓑ 35   Ⓓ 40

Lesson 42
CC.3.NBT.1

1. On Friday, 209 people attended a show. What is 209 rounded to the nearest ten?

  Ⓐ 100
  Ⓑ 200
  Ⓒ 210
  Ⓓ 220

2. There are 852 mystery books in the school library. What is 852 rounded to the nearest ten?

  Ⓐ 800
  Ⓑ 850
  Ⓒ 860
  Ⓓ 900

3. There are 487 books in the classroom library. What is 487 rounded to the nearest ten?

  Ⓐ 480
  Ⓑ 490
  Ⓒ 500
  Ⓓ 510

4. Pizza Place sold 581 pizzas on Friday night. What is 581 rounded to the nearest hundred?

  Ⓐ 600
  Ⓑ 590
  Ⓒ 580
  Ⓓ 500

5. Dan has saved $143. If he rounds $143 to the nearest ten, he gets one number. If he rounds it to the nearest hundred, he gets another number. Explain how one amount can be rounded two different ways.

Possible explanation: $143 rounded to the nearest ten is $140. When $143 is rounded to the nearest hundred, it is $100. Any number can be rounded to the nearest ten or to the nearest hundred.

Lesson 43
CC.3.NBT.1

1. Amber and her friends collected shells. The table shows how many shells each person collected.

Shells Collected

Name	Number of Shells
Amber	372
Melba	455
Pablo	421
Tom	515

Which is the **best** estimate of the total number of shells Amber and Pablo collected?

  Ⓐ 600   Ⓒ 800
  Ⓑ 700   Ⓓ 900

2. The parking lot at the grocery store had 574 parking spaces. Another 128 parking spaces were added to the parking lot. Which is the **best** estimate of the total number of parking spaces in the parking lot now?

  Ⓐ 800   Ⓒ 600
  Ⓑ 700   Ⓓ 500

3. Mavis and her friends collected bottle caps. The table shows how many bottle caps each person collected.

Bottle Caps Collected

Name	Number of Bottle Caps
Karen	372
Mavis	255
Pedro	121
John	315

Which is the **best** estimate of the total number of bottle caps Mavis and Pedro collected?

  Ⓐ 100   Ⓒ 300
  Ⓑ 200   Ⓓ 400

4. Umiko made 47 origami birds last week and 62 origami birds this week. About how many origami birds did she make in the two weeks?

  Ⓐ 10   Ⓒ 110
  Ⓑ 60   Ⓓ 200

5. Bruce wants to use compatible numbers to estimate 173 + 327. Suggest two compatible numbers he could use to estimate the sum. Explain your choices.
Possible answer: 175 + 325; Possible explanation: 173 is close to 175, 327 is close to 325, and 175 and 325 are easy for me to add in my head.

Lesson 44
CC.3.NBT.1

1. Three classes had a reading contest. The table shows how many books the students in each class read.

Reading Contest

Class	Number of Books
Mr. Lopez	273
Ms. Martin	403
Mrs. Wang	147

Which is the **best** estimate of how many more books Ms. Martin's class read than Mr. Lopez's class?

  Ⓐ 100   Ⓒ 300
  Ⓑ 200   Ⓓ 400

2. Abby and Cruz are playing a game. Abby's score is 168 points less than Cruz's score. Cruz's score is 754. Which is the **best** estimate of Abby's score?

  Ⓐ 300   Ⓒ 500
  Ⓑ 400   Ⓓ 600

3. Three classes had a spelling contest. The table shows how many words the students in each class spelled correctly.

Spelling Contest

Class	Number of Words
Mr. Silva	719
Ms. Parker	660
Mrs. Cheng	847

Which is the **best** estimate of how many more words Mrs. Cheng's class spelled correctly than Mr. Silva's class?

  Ⓐ 100   Ⓒ 300
  Ⓑ 200   Ⓓ 400

4. Andre and Salma collect stamps. Andre has 287 stamps. Salma has 95 stamps. About how many more stamps does Andre have than Salma has?

  Ⓐ 400   Ⓒ 200
  Ⓑ 300   Ⓓ 100

5. To estimate 512 − 87, Kim rounded the numbers to 510 − 90 and subtracted. What is another way that Kim could have estimated to subtract? Explain why it might be easier.
Possible explanation: Kim could have used the compatible numbers, 500 and 100. 500 − 100 is easier to subtract mentally than 510 − 90. The estimate would be 400.

Answer Key

1. On Monday, 114 girls and 205 boys wore jeans to school. How many students wore jeans to school on Monday?

Ⓐ 219

Ⓑ 299

Ⓒ 309

● 319

2. The snack stand has 28 honey granola bars and 42 maple granola bars. How many granola bars does the snack stand have in all?

Ⓐ 60

Ⓑ 68

● 70

Ⓓ 78

3. The Smoothie Stop sold 216 banana smoothies and 132 peach smoothies for breakfast. How many banana smoothies and peach smoothies did the Smoothie Stop sell combined?

Ⓐ 358

● 348

Ⓒ 339

Ⓓ 248

4. There are 37 second graders and 27 third graders in the soccer club. How many students are in the soccer club?

Ⓐ 54

● 64

Ⓒ 67

Ⓓ 74

5. Aya has to find the sum of 67 + 34. Explain a mental math strategy she can use to find the sum.

Possible explanation: she can use friendly numbers. She can add 3 to 67 to make 70. Next, she can subtract the 3 from 34 to get 31. Then, she can add 70 + 31 = 101.

---

1. Amy writes a number sentence that shows the Commutative Property of Addition. Which could be Amy's number sentence?

Ⓐ (53 + 9) + 41 = 53 + (9 + 41)

Ⓑ 53 + 0 = 53

Ⓒ 41 = 40 + 1

● 53 + 9 = 9 + 53

2. Mr. Rios bought 24 apples, 16 bananas, and 14 pears at the store. How many pieces of fruit did he buy?

Ⓐ 64

● 54

Ⓒ 40

Ⓓ 38

3. Mario writes a number sentence that shows the Commutative Property of Addition. Which could be Mario's number sentence?

Ⓐ 37 = 36 + 1

Ⓑ 0 + 23 = 23

● 37 + 13 = 13 + 37

Ⓓ (37 + 13) + 23 = 37 + (13 + 23)

4. John writes the following number sentences. Which shows the Associative Property of Addition?

● 7 + (13 + 8) = (7 + 13) + 8

Ⓑ 44 + (56 + 13) = 44 + (13 + 56)

Ⓒ 44 + 56 = 40 + 60

Ⓓ 44 + 56 = 100

5. A ferry carries 47 cars, 28 vans, and 13 trucks to an island. Explain the addition property you would use to find the total number of vehicles on the ferry.

Possible explanation: I'd use the Associative Property to group the addends so they are easy to add. I would look for a group of 10 ones. So first I'd add 47 + 13, which is 60. Then I'd add 60 and 28 to get 88.

---

1. A Rent-A-Raft store rented 213 rafts in June and 455 rafts in July. How many rafts did the Rent-A-Raft store rent in June and July altogether?

Ⓐ 658

● 668

Ⓒ 678

Ⓓ 778

2. Omar wants to break apart the addend 362 to complete an addition problem. Which shows a way to break apart the addend 362?

Ⓐ 3 + 6 + 2

Ⓑ 300 + 60 + 20

Ⓒ 30 + 62

● 300 + 60 + 2

3. Marcus took 242 pictures with his new camera and 155 pictures with his camera phone. How many pictures did Marcus take in all?

● 397

Ⓑ 387

Ⓒ 297

Ⓓ 292

4. The number of campers at Arrowhead Camp was 412 in July and 443 in August. How many campers were at Arrowhead Camp in July and August combined?

Ⓐ 865

● 855

Ⓒ 843

Ⓓ 455

5. Explain how you can tell that the sum of 575 and 338 is greater than 900 without finding the exact sum.

Possible explanation: I know that 575 and 325 make 900, but 325 is less than 338. So when I add 575 and 338, it has to be greater than 900.

---

1. The table shows the number of students visiting the zoo each day.

Field Trips This Week

Day	Number of Students
Monday	346
Tuesday	518
Wednesday	449
Thursday	608

How many students will visit the zoo on Monday and Tuesday combined?

Ⓐ 814   Ⓒ 864

● 854   Ⓓ 964

2. Mr. Rodriguez drove 136 miles to Main City. Then he drove another 146 miles to Rock Town. How many miles did Mr. Rodriguez drive?

Ⓐ 212 miles   Ⓒ 272 miles

Ⓑ 270 miles   ● 282 miles

3. The table shows the number of students who bought lunch in the school cafeteria one week.

Bought Lunch in Cafeteria

Day	Number of Students
Monday	236
Tuesday	319
Wednesday	225
Thursday	284
Friday	306

How many students bought lunch in the cafeteria on Wednesday and Friday combined?

Ⓐ 261   Ⓒ 531

Ⓑ 521   ● 631

4. Mrs. Carlson drove 283 miles to Plant City. She then drove 128 miles to Bond Town. How far did Mrs. Carlson drive?

● 411 miles   Ⓒ 365 miles

Ⓑ 401 miles   Ⓓ 311 miles

5. Bryce has 317 baseball cards. Elin has 168 baseball cards and Jeff has 425 baseball cards. Which two people together have fewer than 500 cards? Explain your answer.

Bryce and Elin; Possible explanation: Jeff has about 400 cards; If I add 400 to either 317 or 168, the sum is greater than 500. So I know it is Bryce and Elin. 317 + 168 is less than 500.

Answer Key

1. Mikio drove a total of 267 miles in 2 days. He drove 125 miles the first day. How many miles did he drive the second day?

(A) 142 miles

(B) 162 miles

(C) 242 miles

(D) 392 miles

2. The Fruity Yogurt Company sold 86 banana yogurt bars and 47 strawberry yogurt bars. How many more banana yogurt bars were sold than strawberry yogurt bars?

(A) 49   (C) 39

(B) 41   (D) 31

3. The Party Popcorn Company sold 58 bags of cheese popcorn and 39 bags of nutty popcorn. How many more bags of cheese popcorn were sold than nutty popcorn?

(A) 97

(B) 41

(C) 29

(D) 19

4. Lin drove a total of 346 miles in 2 days. She drove 204 miles the first day. How many miles did she drive the second day?

(A) 142 miles   (C) 173 miles

(B) 152 miles   (D) 322 miles

5. Kizzy tried to use friendly numbers to subtract 76 − 28. She added 2 to 28 to change it to 30. So she subtracted 2 from 76. Find the error in Kizzy's strategy. Tell how to use friendly numbers to find this difference.

Possible explanation: Kizzy should have added 2 to

both numbers to keep the numbers related in the same

way instead of adding 2 to one number and subtracting

2 from the other. The correct solution is 78 − 30 = 48.

Kizzy's way results in 74 − 30 = 44, which is wrong.

---

1. The school store had 136 notepads. It sold 109 notepads. How many notepads are left?

(A) 27

(B) 33

(C) 37

(D) 43

2. Mr. Ruiz's art students used 159 green beads and 370 orange beads to make necklaces. How many more orange beads than green beads did they use?

(A) 201

(B) 211

(C) 221

(D) 229

3. The craft store had 151 bags of beads. It sold 128 bags. How many bags of beads are left?

(A) 37

(B) 33

(C) 27

(D) 23

4. A movie theater has 245 seats in the main section, and 78 seats up in the balcony. How many more seats are in the main section?

(A) 137

(B) 167

(C) 187

(D) 233

5. Should Ally regroup to subtract 647 − 284? Explain how you know without doing the subtraction. Then tell the steps to find the difference.

Yes; Possible explanation: Ally should regroup a

hundred as 10 tens because there aren't enough tens to

subtract 8 tens. I would subtract the ones. Then I would

regroup 6 hundreds 4 tens as 5 hundreds 14 tens and

subtract the tens. Finally, I would subtract the hundreds.

---

1. Students want to sell 420 tickets to the school fair. They have sold 214 tickets. How many more tickets do they need to sell to reach their goal?

(A) 106

(B) 206

(C) 214

(D) 634

2. A website received 724 visitors last month. This month, there were 953 visitors. How many more visitors did the website have this month than last month?

(A) 1,677   (C) 229

(B) 231   (D) 129

3. The owners of a new discount store expect 350 shoppers the day the store opens. By noon, there are 143 shoppers. How many more shoppers do they need to reach their goal?

(A) 107

(B) 207

(C) 217

(D) 223

4. A popular ride at a theme park has 200 seats. Only 84 people got tickets for the last ride of the day. How many empty seats were there?

(A) 184   (C) 126

(B) 124   (D) 116

5. Neo was asked to find 864 − 557. Explain how he can use the *combine place values* strategy to find the difference.

Possible explanation: he can combine the tens and

ones to think 64 − 57. The difference is 7. He should

record 7 in the ones place and 0 in the tens place.

Then he can subtract the hundreds and record 3.

So, the answer is 307.

---

1. Uncle Tito has 4 nephews. He gives each boy a $30 gift card to a hobby shop. What is the total cost of the 4 gift cards?

(A) $34   (C) $120

(B) $80   (D) $150

2. A toy store has 4 shelves of stuffed animals on display. Each shelf displays 20 stuffed animals. Which diagram shows a way to find the total number of stuffed animals on display?

(A) ▭

(B) ▭

(C) ▭

(D) ▭

3. Wendy buys 7 boxes of envelopes. There are 80 envelopes in each box. How many envelopes does Wendy buy altogether?

(A) 56   (C) 630

(B) 560   (D) 640

4. Aunt Sonya has 5 nieces. She gives each girl a $40 gift card to the museum shop. What is the total cost of the 5 gift cards?

(A) $45

(B) $50

(C) $160

(D) $200

5. Corey sold 5 kites to each of 20 people. How many kites did Corey sell altogether? Explain your answer.

100 kites; Possible explanation: I draw a diagram that shows

5 rows of 20. I know I can break up 5 × 20 into 5 × (10 + 10).

So, I draw a vertical line to show 5 × 10 and another 5 × 10.

5 × 10 = 50, so the product is 50 + 50 or 100.

Answer Key

1. Lucia takes care of farm animals. She works 5 days each week. Last week she took care of 60 farm animals each day she worked. How many farm animals did Lucia take care of last week?

Ⓐ 360   Ⓒ 240

● 300   Ⓓ 65

3. Each school bus has seats for 30 students. On a recent third-grade field trip, 7 buses were filled with students. How many students went on the field trip?

Ⓐ 21   Ⓒ 180

Ⓑ 37   ● 210

2. What multiplication sentence does the model show?

Ⓐ $3 \times 4 = 12$

Ⓑ $2 \times 60 = 120$

● $3 \times 40 = 120$

Ⓓ $4 \times 30 = 120$

4. What multiplication sentence does the model show?

Ⓐ $2 \times 5 = 10$

Ⓑ $3 \times 40 = 120$

● $2 \times 50 = 100$

Ⓓ $2 \times 60 = 120$

5. Mark drew this number line to find 2×60. Explain how Mark can use the number line to find the answer.

0 10 20 30 40 50 60 70 80 90 100 110 120 130 140 150

Possible explanation: 2×60 means 2 groups of 60.

Mark can draw a jump from 0 to 60, and then draw

another jump of 60, which lands on 120. So,

$2 \times 60 = 120$.

---

1. A bank makes rolls of 40 nickels. How many nickels would there be in 8 rolls?

Ⓐ 640

Ⓑ 320

Ⓒ 80

Ⓓ 64

3. Mr. Chandler planted 5 rows of bean seedlings. He planted 50 seedlings in each row. How many seedlings did Mr. Chandler plant?

Ⓐ 55

Ⓑ 200

Ⓒ 250

Ⓓ 350

2. Claire bought 6 bags of beads. There are 80 beads in each bag. How many beads did Claire buy?

● 480

Ⓑ 460

Ⓒ 400

Ⓓ 380

4. Mei-Ling baked 6 batches of rice cakes. There were 30 rice cakes in each batch. How many rice cakes did she bake in all?

Ⓐ 36

Ⓑ 120

Ⓒ 150

● 180

5. One pack of index cards has 80 cards. Explain how to find out how many cards are in 8 packs.

Possible explanation: I know 80 is 8 tens 0 ones.

I multiply the ones: 8×0 ones = 0 ones. Then I multiply

the tens: 8×8 tens = 64 tens. The product is 64 tens

0 ones, which equals 640.

---

1. This shape is divided into equal parts.

What is the name for the parts?

Ⓐ eighths   Ⓒ halves

Ⓑ fourths   ● thirds

3. Jamal folded a piece of cloth into equal parts.

What is the name for the parts?

● eighths   Ⓒ thirds

Ⓑ fourths   Ⓓ halves

2. This shape is divided into equal parts.

What is the number of equal parts?

Ⓐ 8   Ⓒ 3

● 4   Ⓓ 2

4. Kwan folded a circle into equal parts.

What is the name for the parts?

Ⓐ eighths   Ⓒ fourths

● sixths   Ⓓ thirds

5. Hannah has a square cloth. Describe two ways she could divide it into four equal parts.

Possible answer: Hannah could make 4 smaller

squares, or she could draw the diagonals of the

square and form four equal triangles inside it.

---

1. Three friends share 6 graham crackers equally.

How much does each friend get?

● 2 wholes

Ⓑ 2 wholes and 1 half

Ⓒ 3 wholes

Ⓓ 3 wholes and 1 half

3. Four friends share 3 fruit bars equally.

How much does each friend get?

Ⓐ 1 third

Ⓑ 2 thirds

● 3 fourths

Ⓓ 5 eighths

2. Four brothers share 5 cookies equally.

How much does each brother get?

Ⓐ 1 whole and 1 fifth

● 1 whole and 1 fourth

Ⓒ 1 whole and 2 fourths

Ⓓ 1 whole and 4 fifths

4. Three teachers share 7 brownies equally.

How much does each teacher get?

Ⓐ 1 whole and 1 third

Ⓑ 1 whole and 2 thirds

● 2 wholes and 1 third

Ⓓ 2 wholes and 2 thirds

5. Two moms share 3 sandwiches equally.

Shade the squares to show how much each mom gets. Then write the answer.

Possible answers: 1 whole and 1 half, or 3 halves, of a sandwich

Answer Key

1. The shaded part of the model shows how much cornbread was left after dinner.

What fraction of the cornbread was left?

Ⓐ $\frac{1}{3}$ Ⓒ $\frac{1}{6}$

Ⓑ $\frac{1}{4}$ ● $\frac{1}{8}$

3. Kareena made potato salad. She shaded a model to show how much salad was left.

What fraction of the potato salad was left?

Ⓐ $\frac{1}{2}$ Ⓒ $\frac{1}{6}$

● $\frac{1}{4}$ Ⓓ $\frac{1}{8}$

2. Riley shaded a model to show the amount of sandwich she ate.

What fraction of the sandwich did Riley eat?

Ⓐ $\frac{1}{4}$ ● $\frac{1}{2}$

Ⓑ $\frac{1}{3}$ Ⓓ $\frac{1}{1}$

4. The shaded part of the model shows how many paintings were sold at an art show.

What fraction of the paintings were sold?

● $\frac{1}{6}$ Ⓒ $\frac{1}{4}$

Ⓑ $\frac{1}{5}$ Ⓓ $\frac{1}{3}$

5. Mario drew a model to represent $\frac{1}{3}$ of the space in his bookcase. How could Mario draw a model to represent all the space in his bookcase?

Possible answer: because the rectangle represents $\frac{1}{3}$

of the space in his bookshelf, Mario could draw 2 more

rectangles like the one that represented $\frac{1}{3}$.

---

1. What fraction names the shaded part of the page?

Ⓐ eight sixths

Ⓑ eight eighths

● six eighths

Ⓓ two sixths

3. What fraction names the shaded part of the shape?

Ⓐ three eighths

● five eighths

Ⓒ six eighths

Ⓓ eight eighths

2. Lilly shaded this model to show what part of all the books she read are fiction.

What fraction of the books Lilly read are fiction?

Ⓐ $\frac{3}{3}$ Ⓒ $\frac{3}{4}$

Ⓑ $\frac{5}{6}$ ● $\frac{3}{6}$

4. Bailey shaded this model to show what part of all the baseball games his team won last season.

What fraction of the games did Bailey's team win?

Ⓐ $\frac{2}{6}$ ● $\frac{4}{6}$

Ⓑ $\frac{2}{4}$ Ⓓ $\frac{6}{4}$

5. Ashleigh shaded a model to show what part of the bracelets she made are blue. Explain how the model can be used to describe what part of the bracelets Ashleigh made are not blue.

Possible answer: 3 parts are not shaded, so three fourths

describes the part of the bracelets that are not blue.

---

1. There are 8 rows of chairs in the auditorium. Three of the rows are empty. What fraction of the rows of chairs are empty?

Ⓐ $\frac{5}{8}$ Ⓒ $\frac{3}{8}$

Ⓑ $\frac{4}{8}$ Ⓓ $\frac{1}{8}$

3. David sold 6 apple trees. He sold 5 of the apple trees to Max. What fraction of the apple trees did David sell to Max?

Ⓐ $\frac{1}{6}$ ● $\frac{5}{6}$

Ⓑ $\frac{3}{16}$ Ⓓ $\frac{6}{5}$

2. Greyson has 3 baseballs. He brings 2 baseballs to school. What fraction of his baseballs does Greyson bring to school?

Ⓐ $\frac{1}{3}$ ● $\frac{2}{3}$

Ⓑ $\frac{1}{2}$ Ⓓ $\frac{3}{2}$

4. Maria has 8 tulip bulbs. She gives 3 of the tulip bulbs to her neighbor. What fraction of her tulip bulbs does Maria give to her neighbor?

● $\frac{3}{8}$ Ⓒ $\frac{3}{5}$

Ⓑ $\frac{5}{8}$ Ⓓ $\frac{8}{3}$

5. Diana writes $\frac{1}{4}$ to describe the group of balloons shown below. What could Diana be describing? Explain your reasoning.

Possible answer: Diana is describing the gray part of the

set. The denominator stands for the 4 parts of the group.

The numerator stands for 1 part of the group.

---

1. Charlotte bought 16 songs. One fourth of the songs are pop songs.

How many of the songs are pop songs?

Ⓐ 16   ● 4

Ⓑ 12   Ⓓ 1

3. Mr. Walton ordered 12 pizzas for the art class celebration. One fourth of the pizzas had only mushrooms.

How many of the pizzas had only mushrooms?

Ⓐ 1   Ⓒ 4

● 3   Ⓓ 9

2. Sophie uses 18 beads to make a necklace. One sixth of the beads are purple. How many of the beads are purple?

Ⓐ 1   Ⓒ 6

● 3   Ⓓ 18

4. Caleb took 24 photos at the zoo. One eighth of his photos are of giraffes. How many of Caleb's photos are of giraffes?

Ⓐ 1   Ⓒ 8

● 3   Ⓓ 24

5. Mrs. Green bought 15 plants. One third of them were tomato plants. Mrs. Green said she bought 5 tomato plants. Do you agree? Explain your answer.

I agree; Possible explanation: I divided 15 counters into

3 groups. Then I counted the number in one of the 3

groups. There were 5 counters in the group.

Answer Key

1. Samuel brought 2 autographed baseballs for show and tell. They are $\frac{1}{6}$ of his whole collection. How many autographed baseballs are in Samuel's whole collection?

  (A) 3   (C) 12

  (B) 4   (D) 13

2. Together, Dillon and Leon make up $\frac{1}{4}$ of the midfielders on the soccer team. How many midfielders are on the team?

  (A) 2   (C) 6

  (B) 4   (D) 8

3. Ben has 12 model cars in his room. These cars represent $\frac{1}{2}$ of the model cars in Ben's whole collection. How many model cars does Ben have in his whole collection?

  (A) 24   (C) 15

  (B) 18   (D) 6

4. A garden has 2 yellow rose plants. These rose plants represent $\frac{1}{8}$ of the plants in the entire garden. How many plants are in the entire garden?

  (A) 4   (C) 10

  (B) 6   (D) 16

5. Laura found 5 shells on a trip to the beach. These shells represent $\frac{1}{3}$ of the shells in her whole collection. How many shells does Laura have in her whole collection? Draw a diagram to find the answer.

15 shells; Possible drawings are shown.

Number and Operations–Fractions   61

1. Which fraction names point A on the number line?

  (A) $\frac{1}{8}$ (C) $\frac{7}{8}$

  (B) $\frac{6}{8}$ (D) $\frac{8}{8}$

2. Which fraction names point A on the number line?

  (A) $\frac{1}{6}$ (C) $\frac{3}{6}$

  (B) $\frac{2}{6}$ (D) $\frac{1}{1}$

3. Lucy can ride her bike around the block 4 times for a total of 1 mile. How many times will she ride around the block to go $\frac{3}{4}$ mile?

  (A) 2   (C) 6

  (B) 3   (D) 8

4. Carlos can walk around the track 8 times for a total of 1 mile. How many times will he walk around the track to go $\frac{7}{8}$ mile?

  (A) 1   (C) 5

  (B) 3   (D) 7

5. Fruit bars come 3 bars to a package. Explain how to use the number line to find how many fruit bars Tara would eat to finish $\frac{2}{3}$ of a package.

Possible answer: each fruit bar represents $\frac{1}{3}$ of a package. Two bars represent $\frac{2}{3}$ of a package. Tara would eat 2 fruit bars.

62   Number and Operations–Fractions

1. Brenda paints $\frac{1}{2}$ of a wall green.

Which fraction is equivalent to $\frac{1}{2}$?

  (A) $\frac{4}{8}$ (C) $\frac{2}{1}$

  (B) $\frac{1}{6}$ (D) $\frac{2}{6}$

2. Maria has $\frac{1}{2}$ of an obstacle course left to finish.

Which fraction is equivalent to $\frac{1}{2}$?

  (A) $\frac{2}{1}$ (C) $\frac{3}{6}$

  (B) $\frac{2}{6}$ (D) $\frac{5}{6}$

3. Ming-Na has read $\frac{2}{3}$ of a book. Glenn has read the same amount of the book.

Which fraction is equivalent to $\frac{2}{3}$?

  (A) $\frac{1}{2}$ (C) $\frac{3}{4}$

  (B) $\frac{5}{8}$ (D) $\frac{4}{6}$

4. Mrs. Reid needs $\frac{3}{4}$ cup of brown sugar for a recipe.

Which fraction is equivalent to $\frac{3}{4}$?

  (A) $\frac{7}{8}$ (C) $\frac{3}{8}$

  (B) $\frac{6}{8}$ (D) $\frac{4}{3}$

5. Use the fraction circles to complete the statement.

$$\frac{1}{4} = \frac{\boxed{2}}{8}$$

Explain how the numerators and denominators are related in the equivalent fractions.
Possible answer: the numerator and denominator in $\frac{2}{8}$ are both double the numerator and denominator in $\frac{1}{4}$.

Number and Operations—Fractions   63

1. Sam went for a ride on a sailboat. The ride lasted $\frac{3}{4}$ hour.

Which fraction is equivalent to $\frac{3}{4}$?

  (A) $\frac{3}{6}$ (C) $\frac{3}{8}$

  (B) $\frac{4}{8}$ (D) $\frac{6}{8}$

2. Tom rode his horse for $\frac{4}{6}$ mile. Liz rode her horse for an equal distance.

Which fraction is equivalent to $\frac{4}{6}$?

  (A) $\frac{1}{3}$ (C) $\frac{2}{6}$

  (B) $\frac{2}{3}$ (D) $\frac{4}{3}$

3. Pedro is doing his math homework. He has completed $\frac{8}{8}$ of the problems. Which fraction is equivalent to $\frac{8}{8}$?

  (A) $\frac{0}{8}$ (C) $\frac{6}{6}$

  (B) $\frac{1}{8}$ (D) $\frac{3}{6}$

4. Aaron is planting a vegetable garden. He made room in $\frac{1}{4}$ of his garden for beans. Which shape has a shaded part equivalent to $\frac{1}{4}$?

  (A)   (C)

  (B)   (D)

5. Danielle's model shows $\frac{1}{2} = \frac{2}{4}$. Describe a different way you could circle equal groups to show another equivalent fraction. Explain how you know your fraction is equivalent to $\frac{1}{2}$ and $\frac{2}{4}$.

Possible answer: I can circle two equal groups of 4. Each group has 4 parts. I know that $\frac{4}{8}$ is equivalent to $\frac{1}{2}$ and $\frac{2}{4}$ because they are all the same size on the model.

64   Number and Operations—Fractions

Answer Key

1. Which numbers from the number line are equal?

ⓐ $\frac{6}{6}$ and 1   ⓒ $\frac{0}{6}$ and 1

ⓑ $\frac{3}{6}$ and $\frac{6}{6}$ ⓓ $\frac{0}{6}$ and $\frac{6}{6}$

2. Cora cuts the apple pies into equal parts.

What fraction greater than 1 names both apple pies?

ⓐ $\frac{2}{6}$ ⓒ $\frac{6}{6}$

ⓑ $\frac{6}{12}$ ⓓ $\frac{12}{6}$

3. Emma colored some shapes. What fraction greater than 1 names the parts that she shaded?

ⓐ $\frac{6}{2}$ ⓒ $\frac{2}{3}$

ⓑ $\frac{6}{3}$ ⓓ $\frac{2}{6}$

4. Mr. Angelo sliced two pizzas into equal parts.

What fraction greater than 1 names both pizzas?

ⓐ $\frac{2}{16}$ ⓒ $\frac{16}{8}$

ⓑ $\frac{8}{16}$ ⓓ $\frac{16}{4}$

5. Greg painted three circles. He wrote the fraction $\frac{3}{24}$ for the shaded parts.

Is Greg correct? Explain your answer.
No; Possible answer: each whole is divided into 8 equal parts so the denominator should be 8. He shaded a total of 24 parts so the numerator should be 24: $\frac{24}{8}$.

---

1. Bill used $\frac{1}{3}$ cup of raisins and $\frac{2}{3}$ cup of banana chips to make a snack. Which statement correctly compares the fractions?

ⓐ $\frac{1}{3} > \frac{2}{3}$ ⓒ $\frac{2}{3} > \frac{1}{3}$

ⓑ $\frac{2}{3} < \frac{1}{3}$ ⓓ $\frac{2}{3} = \frac{1}{3}$

2. Mavis mixed $\frac{1}{4}$ quart of red paint with $\frac{3}{4}$ quart of yellow paint to make orange paint. Which of the following statements is **true**?

Ⓐ Mavis used less yellow paint than red paint.

Ⓑ Mavis used more red paint than yellow paint.

Ⓒ Mavis used equal amounts of red and yellow paint.

Ⓓ Mavis used more yellow paint than red paint.

3. Carlos found that $\frac{1}{2}$ of the apples in one basket are Granny Smith apples and $\frac{1}{6}$ of the apples in another basket are Granny Smith apples. The baskets are the same size. Which statement correctly compares the fractions?

ⓐ $\frac{1}{2} = \frac{1}{6}$ ⓒ $\frac{1}{2} > \frac{1}{6}$

ⓑ $\frac{1}{2} < \frac{1}{6}$ ⓓ $\frac{1}{6} > \frac{1}{2}$

4. Of the stars on the Monroe Elementary School flag, $\frac{2}{4}$ are gold and $\frac{2}{8}$ are black. Which statement correctly compares the fractions?

ⓐ $\frac{2}{8} > \frac{2}{4}$ ⓒ $\frac{2}{4} = \frac{2}{8}$

ⓑ $\frac{2}{8} < \frac{2}{4}$ ⓓ $\frac{2}{4} < \frac{2}{8}$

5. Tess ate $\frac{3}{8}$ of her granola bar. Gino ate $\frac{3}{4}$ of his granola bar. Both granola bars were the same size. Who ate more? Describe how you could use fraction strips to solve the problem.
Gino; Possible answer: I could model $\frac{3}{8}$ and $\frac{3}{4}$ and compare the lengths. The length of the $\frac{3}{4}$ model would be greater than the length of the $\frac{3}{8}$ model, so $\frac{3}{4}$ is greater than $\frac{3}{8}$.

---

1. Dan and David are on the track team. Dan runs $\frac{1}{4}$ mile each day. David runs $\frac{3}{4}$ mile each day. Which statement is correct?

Ⓐ David runs farther than Dan each day.

Ⓑ David runs more than 1 mile each day.

Ⓒ David runs the same distance as Dan each day.

Ⓓ Dan runs farther than David each day.

2. Isabel and Raul are playing a game with fraction circles. Which statement is correct?

ⓐ $\frac{1}{3} > \frac{2}{3}$ ⓒ $\frac{2}{3} < \frac{1}{3}$

ⓑ $\frac{2}{3} = \frac{1}{3}$ ⓓ $\frac{2}{3} > \frac{1}{3}$

3. Chun lives $\frac{3}{8}$ mile from the library. Gail lives $\frac{5}{8}$ mile from the library. Which statement is correct?

Ⓐ Chun lives more than 1 mile from the library.

Ⓑ Chun lives farther from the library than Gail.

Ⓒ Gail lives farther from the library than Chun.

Ⓓ Gail and Chun live the same distance from the library.

4. Students are making quilt squares. They want $\frac{2}{6}$ of the quilt squares to be red and $\frac{4}{6}$ of the quilt squares to be white. Which statement correctly compares the fractions?

ⓐ $\frac{2}{6} = \frac{4}{6}$ ⓒ $\frac{4}{6} < \frac{2}{6}$

ⓑ $\frac{2}{6} < \frac{4}{6}$ ⓓ $\frac{2}{6} > \frac{4}{6}$

5. Kevin and Trevor each have a small pizza. Kevin eats $\frac{5}{6}$ of his pizza and Trevor eats $\frac{4}{6}$ of his pizza. Who eats the lesser amount? Explain how to use fraction circles to compare the fractions.
Trevor; Possible explanation: I would use 2 fraction circles divided into sixths. 4 shaded parts is less than 5, so Trevor eats less pizza than Kevin.

---

1. Jenna ate $\frac{1}{8}$ of one pizza. Mark ate $\frac{1}{6}$ of another pizza. The pizzas are the same size. Which statement correctly compares the amount of pizza that was eaten?

ⓐ $\frac{1}{6} < \frac{1}{8}$ ⓒ $\frac{1}{8} > \frac{1}{6}$

ⓑ $\frac{1}{8} = \frac{1}{6}$ ⓓ $\frac{1}{8} < \frac{1}{6}$

2. Jacob and Ella are reading the same book. Jacob read $\frac{5}{8}$ of the book. Ella read $\frac{5}{6}$ of the book. Which statement is correct?

Ⓐ Jacob read more of the book than Ella.

Ⓑ Ella read less of the book than Jacob.

Ⓒ Jacob read less of the book than Ella.

Ⓓ Ella and Jacob read the same amount of the book.

3. In a survey, $\frac{1}{3}$ of the students chose soccer as their favorite sport and $\frac{1}{4}$ chose basketball. Which statement correctly compares the fractions?

ⓐ $\frac{1}{3} < \frac{1}{4}$ ⓒ $\frac{1}{3} > \frac{1}{4}$

ⓑ $\frac{1}{3} = \frac{1}{4}$ ⓓ $\frac{1}{4} > \frac{1}{3}$

4. Maria put $\frac{3}{4}$ yard of fringe around the pillow she made. Nancy put $\frac{3}{8}$ yard of fringe around her pillow. Which statement correctly compares the fractions?

ⓐ $\frac{3}{4} > \frac{3}{8}$
ⓑ $\frac{3}{4} < \frac{3}{8}$
ⓒ $\frac{3}{4} = \frac{3}{8}$
ⓓ $\frac{3}{8} > \frac{3}{4}$

5. Rory can either have $\frac{2}{6}$ of a cheese pizza or $\frac{2}{8}$ of a vegetable pizza. The pizzas are the same size. Rory wants to eat the smaller amount of pizza. Which type of pizza should Rory eat? Explain your answer.
the vegetable pizza; Possible explanation: the denominators show the number of equal parts. The pizza with 8 equal parts has smaller slices than the pizza with 6 equal parts. So, $\frac{2}{8}$ is less than $\frac{2}{6}$.

1. Floyd caught a fish that weighed $\frac{3}{4}$ pound. Kevin caught a fish that weighed $\frac{2}{3}$ pound. Which statement is correct?

   Ⓐ $\frac{3}{4} > \frac{2}{3}$

   Ⓑ $\frac{3}{4} < \frac{2}{3}$

   Ⓒ $\frac{2}{3} = \frac{3}{4}$

   Ⓓ $\frac{2}{3} > \frac{3}{4}$

2. There are two nature walks around the park. One trail is $\frac{7}{8}$ mile long. The other trail is $\frac{4}{8}$ mile long. Which statement is correct?

   Ⓐ $\frac{7}{8} < \frac{4}{8}$

   Ⓑ $\frac{7}{8} = \frac{4}{8}$

   Ⓒ $\frac{4}{8} < \frac{7}{8}$

   Ⓓ $\frac{4}{8} > \frac{7}{8}$

3. Olga is making play dough. She starts by mixing $\frac{1}{8}$ cup of salt with $\frac{1}{3}$ cup of water. Which statement is correct?

   Ⓐ $\frac{1}{8} = \frac{1}{3}$

   Ⓑ $\frac{1}{8} < \frac{1}{3}$

   Ⓒ $\frac{1}{8} > \frac{1}{3}$

   Ⓓ $\frac{1}{3} < \frac{1}{8}$

4. Kyle and Kelly planted seedlings. Kyle's plant is $\frac{5}{6}$ inch tall. Kelly's plant is $\frac{5}{8}$ inch tall. Which statement is correct?

   Ⓐ $\frac{5}{8} > \frac{5}{6}$

   Ⓑ $\frac{5}{8} = \frac{5}{6}$

   Ⓒ $\frac{5}{6} < \frac{5}{8}$

   Ⓓ $\frac{5}{6} > \frac{5}{8}$

5. Lynne and Crosby are meeting at the school playground. Lynne lives $\frac{4}{5}$ mile from the playground. Crosby lives $\frac{5}{6}$ mile from the playground. Who lives closer to the playground? Explain how you found your answer.

   Lynne; Possible explanation: I can use the missing pieces

   strategy to compare the fractions because each fraction is

   missing one piece to make a whole. $\frac{4}{5}$ will have a larger missing

   piece than $\frac{5}{6}$, so $\frac{4}{5} < \frac{5}{6}$, and is closer to the playground.

Number and Operations—Fractions   69

---

1. Pat, Elina, and Mike are meeting at the library. Pat lives $\frac{3}{4}$ mile from the library. Elina lives $\frac{1}{4}$ mile from the library. Mike lives $\frac{2}{4}$ mile from the library. Which list orders the fractions from **least** to **greatest**?

   Ⓐ $\frac{2}{4}, \frac{1}{4}, \frac{3}{4}$

   Ⓑ $\frac{1}{4}, \frac{3}{4}, \frac{2}{4}$

   Ⓒ $\frac{1}{4}, \frac{2}{4}, \frac{3}{4}$

   Ⓓ $\frac{3}{4}, \frac{2}{4}, \frac{1}{4}$

2. Ming is painting a picture. He has $\frac{2}{3}$ pint of red paint, $\frac{2}{8}$ pint of yellow paint, and $\frac{2}{6}$ pint of green paint. Which list orders the fractions from **greatest** to **least**?

   Ⓐ $\frac{2}{3}, \frac{2}{8}, \frac{2}{6}$

   Ⓑ $\frac{2}{3}, \frac{2}{6}, \frac{2}{8}$

   Ⓒ $\frac{2}{8}, \frac{2}{6}, \frac{2}{3}$

   Ⓓ $\frac{2}{6}, \frac{2}{3}, \frac{2}{8}$

3. Brian is making coconut bars. He needs $\frac{1}{3}$ cup coconut flakes, $\frac{1}{4}$ cup milk, and $\frac{1}{2}$ cup flour. Which list orders the fractions from **least** to **greatest**?

   Ⓐ $\frac{1}{4}, \frac{1}{3}, \frac{1}{2}$

   Ⓑ $\frac{1}{2}, \frac{1}{3}, \frac{1}{4}$

   Ⓒ $\frac{1}{4}, \frac{1}{2}, \frac{1}{3}$

   Ⓓ $\frac{1}{3}, \frac{1}{4}, \frac{1}{2}$

4. Cora measures the heights of three plants. The first plant is $\frac{4}{4}$ foot tall. The second plant is $\frac{4}{8}$ foot tall. The third plant is $\frac{4}{6}$ foot tall. Which list orders the fractions from **greatest** to **least**?

   Ⓐ $\frac{4}{4}, \frac{4}{6}, \frac{4}{8}$

   Ⓑ $\frac{4}{6}, \frac{4}{8}, \frac{4}{4}$

   Ⓒ $\frac{4}{8}, \frac{4}{6}, \frac{4}{4}$

   Ⓓ $\frac{4}{4}, \frac{4}{8}, \frac{4}{6}$

5. Gina measured the heights of three seedlings. The heights were $\frac{3}{8}$ inch, $\frac{3}{4}$ inch, and $\frac{3}{6}$ inch. Explain how Gina can compare and order the heights, from least to greatest, of the seedlings she measured.

   Possible answer: the heights of Gina's seedlings all

   have the same numerator, so she can compare the

   denominators to order the heights. The seedling with the

   greatest denominator is the shortest and the seedling

   with the least denominator is the tallest.

70   Number and Operations—Fractions

---

1. Brad looked at the clock on his way to football practice.

   What time is shown on Brad's clock?

   Ⓐ thirteen minutes before nine

   Ⓑ thirteen minutes after nine

   Ⓒ nine forty-five

   Ⓓ thirteen minutes before ten

2. Sarah looked at her watch before she began mowing the grass. The hour hand was between the 9 and the 10. The minute hand was on the 7. At what time did Sarah begin mowing the grass?

   Ⓐ 7:09   Ⓒ 9:07

   Ⓑ 7:10   Ⓓ 9:35

3. Chris looked at his watch before he began raking the leaves. The hour hand was between the 10 and the 11. The minute hand was on the 5. At what time did Chris begin raking the leaves?

   Ⓐ 10:25   Ⓒ 5:11

   Ⓑ 10:05   Ⓓ 5:10

4. Jillian checked the clock before she began piano practice.

   4:27

   What time is shown on Jillian's clock?

   Ⓐ four twenty-five

   Ⓑ twenty-seven minutes after four

   Ⓒ three minutes before five

   Ⓓ twenty-seven minutes before five

5. What time is it on a clock when the two hands form a straight line between 12 and 6? Explain.

   6:00; possible explanation: the minute hand would point

   to 12 and the hour hand to 6. It is 6:00 and not 12:30

   because at 12:30, the hour hand is not straight up but

   halfway between 12 and 1.

Measurement and Data   71

---

1. Keisha is eating dinner at quarter after 6:00. At what time is Keisha eating dinner?

   Ⓐ 5:45 A.M.

   Ⓑ 6:15 A.M.

   Ⓒ 5:45 P.M.

   Ⓓ 6:15 P.M.

2. Terry went fishing at 6 minutes past 7:00 in the morning. At what time did Terry go fishing?

   Ⓐ 6:07 A.M.

   Ⓑ 7:06 A.M.

   Ⓒ 6:07 P.M.

   Ⓓ 7:06 P.M.

3. Ricardo wakes up at quarter to 7:00 in the morning. At what time does Ricardo wake up?

   Ⓐ 6:45 A.M.

   Ⓑ 7:15 A.M.

   Ⓒ 6:45 P.M.

   Ⓓ 7:15 P.M.

4. Makati's class begins social studies at 10 minutes after 1:00 in the afternoon. At what time does social studies begin?

   Ⓐ 1:10 A.M.

   Ⓑ 10:01 A.M.

   Ⓒ 1:10 P.M.

   Ⓓ 10:01 P.M.

5. Charlie has a guitar lesson at 2:00. Is that time likely to be A.M. or P.M.? Explain.

   P.M.; possible explanation: A.M. is after midnight and in the

   morning until noontime. P.M. is after noon and through

   the evening. A guitar lesson would not be 2 hours after

   midnight, which is when people are sleeping. It is 2:00 in

   the afternoon.

72   Measurement and Data

Answer Key

123

1. Arianna started reading her book at 11:20 A.M. and stopped reading her book at 11:43 A.M. For how long did Arianna read her book?

Ⓐ 23 minutes
Ⓑ 28 minutes
Ⓒ 33 minutes
Ⓓ 63 minutes

2. Hector left to take a walk at 6:25 P.M. He returned home at 6:51 P.M. How long was Hector's walk?

Ⓐ 16 minutes
Ⓑ 21 minutes
● 26 minutes
Ⓓ 76 minutes

3. Victoria started her spelling homework at 4:25 P.M. and finished at 4:37 P.M. How long did it take Victoria to complete her spelling homework?

Ⓐ 27 minutes
Ⓑ 22 minutes
Ⓒ 17 minutes
Ⓓ 12 minutes

4. Cheung started playing basketball at 9:17 A.M. He stopped playing at 9:45 A.M. How long did Cheung play basketball?

Ⓐ 28 minutes   Ⓒ 38 minutes
Ⓑ 32 minutes   Ⓓ 42 minutes

5. Magda worked on a computer from 1:40 P.M. to 2:14 P.M. Explain how you know whether she worked on the computer for more or less than 30 minutes.

Possible explanation: 30 minutes after 1:40 would be 2:10.

Magda was on the computer until 2:14, which comes after

2:10. She worked for 34 minutes, which is more than

30 minutes.

Measurement and Data   73

---

1. Jai's piano lesson started at 4:35 P.M. The lesson lasted 45 minutes. What time did Jai's piano lesson end?

Ⓐ 3:50 P.M.
Ⓑ 5:10 P.M.
Ⓒ 5:20 P.M.
Ⓓ 5:35 P.M.

2. Ky was at the skateboard park for 35 minutes. He left the park at 3:10 P.M. What time did Ky arrive at the skateboard park?

Ⓐ 2:35 P.M.
Ⓑ 2:40 P.M.
Ⓒ 2:45 P.M.
Ⓓ 3:45 P.M.

3. A batch of muffins needs to bake for 22 minutes. Wade puts the muffins in the oven at 10:17 A.M. At what time should Wade take the muffins out of the oven?

Ⓐ 10:29 A.M.
● 10:39 A.M.
Ⓒ 10:49 A.M.
Ⓓ 10:55 A.M.

4. Yul's art class started at 11:25 A.M. The class lasted 30 minutes. At what time did Yul's art class end?

Ⓐ 10:55 A.M.
Ⓑ 11:35 A.M.
Ⓒ 11:50 A.M.
● 11:55 A.M.

5. Delia started her project at 9:30 A.M. and finished at 10:10 A.M. Colin finished his project at 10:45 A.M. Both students worked for the same amount of time. What time did Colin start his project? Explain how you know.

10:05; possible explanation: first, I figured out that Delia

worked for 40 minutes. Then, I counted back 40 minutes

from 10:45, which is 10:05.

74   Measurement and Data

---

1. Omar rode his bike in the park for 45 minutes and rode in his neighborhood for 25 minutes. Omar stopped riding his bike at 4:40 P.M.

At what time did Omar start riding his bike?

Ⓐ 4:15 P.M.   Ⓒ 3:40 P.M.
Ⓑ 3:55 P.M.   ● 3:30 P.M.

2. Sophia folded laundry for 25 minutes. After folding laundry, she worked on a puzzle for 42 minutes. Sophia began folding laundry at 8:20 A.M. At what time did Sophia stop working on the puzzle?

Ⓐ 7:13 A.M.   Ⓒ 9:27 A.M.
Ⓑ 9:02 A.M.   Ⓓ 9:32 A.M.

3. Cheerleading practice started at 3:10 P.M. During practice, Dina practiced tumbling for 15 minutes. Then she practiced cheers for 35 minutes.

At what time did Dina's cheerleading practice end?

Ⓐ 3:25 P.M.   ● 4:00 P.M.
Ⓑ 3:45 P.M.   Ⓓ 4:15 P.M.

4. Mr. Carver spent 45 minutes making dinner. Then, he spent 18 minutes eating dinner. He finished eating at 6:15 P.M. At what time did Mr. Carver start making dinner?

● 5:12 P.M.   Ⓒ 5:30 P.M.
Ⓑ 5:22 P.M.   Ⓓ 6:12 P.M.

5. Karl did his chores for 25 minutes. Then he read for 15 minutes. He finished reading at 5:20 P.M. Explain how you can find the time he began his chores.

Possible explanation: I can combine 25 and 15 minutes, which

is 40 minutes in all. Then I count backward on a clock

40 minutes, which is 20 minutes before 5:00 or 4:40 P.M.

Measurement and Data   75

---

1. There are four bottles of punch on a shelf. The bottles are all the same size. Which bottle has the least amount of punch?

Ⓐ Bottle Q   Ⓒ Bottle S
Ⓑ Bottle R   Ⓓ Bottle T

2. Meiki fills a mug with hot cocoa. Which is the best estimate of how much she poured into the mug?

Ⓐ about 1 liter
Ⓑ less than 1 liter
Ⓒ more than 1 liter
Ⓓ about 5 liters

3. There are four bottles of juice on the counter. The bottles are all the same size. Which bottle has the greatest amount of juice?

Ⓐ Bottle A   Ⓒ Bottle C
Ⓑ Bottle B   Ⓓ Bottle D

4. Jed fills a bucket with water to wash the floor. Which is the best estimate of how much water he put in the bucket?

Ⓐ a lot less than a liter
Ⓑ a little less than a liter
Ⓒ about a liter
Ⓓ more than a liter

5. A soup pot and a water bottle are the same height. Which one will hold more liquid? Explain.

soup pot; possible explanation: liquid volume depends

on height and width of the container. The soup pot would

be wider, although the same height, so it probably holds

more liquid.

76   Measurement and Data

Answer Key

Lesson 77
CC.3.MD.2

Name _____

1. Ling uses grams to measure the mass of an object in her room. Which object would be **best** measured using grams?

Ⓐ   glasses

Ⓑ desk

Ⓒ book

Ⓓ bed

2. Kylie wants to find the mass of a pair of her sneakers. Which unit should she use?

Ⓐ liter Ⓒ inch

Ⓑ kilogram Ⓓ gram

3. Jason uses a balance to compare the masses of the objects shown. What is true about the objects?

Ⓐ The mass of the erasers is the same as the mass of the paper clips.

Ⓑ The mass of the erasers is less than the mass of the paper clips.

Ⓒ The mass of the paper clips is less than the mass of the erasers.

Ⓓ The mass of the paper clips is greater than the mass of the erasers.

4. Stav adopted a puppy. The data sheet for the puppy gave its mass as 2, but left off the unit. What unit makes sense? Explain your thinking.

Kilograms; possible explanation: the units of mass I know are gram and kilogram. A puppy of 2 grams would be about the same as 2 paper clips, which is too small. So, the puppy would have a mass of 2 kilograms.

Measurement and Data   77

Lesson 78
CC.3.MD.2

Name _____

1. Bryce has a container completely filled with 13 liters of water. Ben has a container completely filled with 8 liters of water. What is the total liquid volume of the containers?

Ⓐ 5 liters Ⓒ 21 liters

Ⓑ 11 liters Ⓓ 24 liters

2. An online company shipped three packages. The packages had masses of 8 kilograms, 15 kilograms, and 9 kilograms. What is the total mass of the three packages?

Ⓐ 23 kilograms

Ⓑ 24 kilograms

Ⓒ 32 kilograms

Ⓓ 34 kilograms

3. Mama's Restaurant sold a total of 15 liters of orange juice in 3 hours. The same amount of orange juice was sold each hour. How many liters of orange juice were sold each hour?

Ⓐ 5 liters Ⓒ 18 liters

Ⓑ 12 liters Ⓓ 45 liters

4. Simon pours 19 liters of water into one bucket and 15 liters of water into another bucket. Each bucket is filled completely. What is the total liquid volume of the two buckets?

Ⓐ 4 liters

Ⓑ 14 liters

Ⓒ 24 liters

Ⓓ 34 liters

5. At a football game, the Pep Club sold a total of 18 liters of fruit punch in 2 hours. The same amount of fruit punch was sold each hour. Explain how to find the amount of fruit punch that was sold each hour.

Possible explanation: this is a division problem; a total of 18 liters needs to be divided into 2 equal parts. I can use a bar model to show the two equal parts that make up the whole. 18 ÷ 2 is 9, so 9 liters of punch were sold each hour.

78   Measurement and Data

Lesson 79
CC.3.MD.3

Name _____

Use the table for 1–2.

Mike asked people what season they liked best. The tally table shows the results.

Favorite Season	
Winter	⦀ ⫴
Spring	⦀ ⦀ ⎮
Summer	⎜⎜⎜⎜
Fall	⦀

1. How many people chose Winter or Summer?

Ⓐ 4 Ⓒ 11

Ⓑ 10 Ⓓ 12

2. How many **more** students chose Spring than Fall?

Ⓐ 4 Ⓒ 6

Ⓑ 5 Ⓓ 11

Use the table for 3–4.

Rory and his classmates voted for a favorite class activity. They organized the data in a tally table.

Favorite Class Activity	
Science Fair	⦀ ⦀
Bake Sale	⎜⎜⎜⎜
Fitness Fun Day	⦀ ⦀ ⎜⎜
Class Play	⦀ ⎜⎜⎜⎜

3. How many students chose the Science Fair or Fitness Fun Day?

Ⓐ 6 Ⓒ 20

Ⓑ 12 Ⓓ 22

4. How many **fewer** students chose a Bake Sale than Fitness Fun Day?

Ⓐ 4 Ⓒ 10

Ⓑ 8 Ⓓ 12

5. Dan asked 24 members of his class how they traveled to their last vacation spot. The frequency table shows the results. Complete the table and explain how you did it.

Travel Vehicle	Boys	Girls
Car	4	4
Airplane	6	5
Bus	2	3

I added the numbers in the table for both girls and boys. I subtracted the total, 20, from 24, and wrote 4 in the blank box.

Measurement and Data   79

Lesson 80
CC.3.MD.3

Name _____

1. Ms. Sanchez's class took pictures of a lighthouse during a field trip. The picture graph shows how many pictures each student took.

Lighthouse Pictures	
Gerald	⬡⬡⬡⬡⬡
Yung	⬡⬡⬡⬡⬡⬡⬡
Ramesh	⬡⬡
Jose	⬡⬡⬡⬡⬡⬡⬡⬡⬡⬡

Key: Each ⬡ = 2 pictures.

How many pictures were taken in all?

Ⓐ 28 Ⓒ 52

Ⓑ 32 Ⓓ 56

2. The picture graph shows the number of bottles Mr. Tao's class recycled each week for an Earth Day project.

Weekly Bottle Recycling	
Week 1	
Week 2	
Week 3	
Week 4	

Key: Each = 10 bottles.

How many bottles were recycled during Week 2 and Week 3?

Ⓐ 9 Ⓒ 85

Ⓑ 14 Ⓓ 140

3. Mrs. Hampton's class made a picture graph to show the type of material used to make each picture at an art show.

Pictures at the Art Show	
Chalk	▯▯▯▯▯
Crayon	▯▯▯▯
Paint	▯▯▯▯▯▯▯

Key: Each ▮ = 2 pictures.

How many **fewer** pictures were made with crayon than with paint?

Ⓐ 4 Ⓒ 9

Ⓑ 5 Ⓓ 12

4. Pam tossed a coin 20 times and made a picture graph of her data.

Coin Toss Results	
Heads	○○○○
Tails	○○○○○○

Key: Each ○ = 2 coin tosses.

Explain how the picture graph would be different if each circle represented 4 coin tosses.

There would be 2 circles for Heads and 3 circles for Tails. The key would show that a circle represents 4 tosses instead of 2 tosses.

80   Measurement and Data

Answer Key

Lesson 81
CC.3.MD.3

Name _____

Use the table for 1–2.

Kim did a survey to learn which pet her classmates liked best. She wrote the results in a table and will use the data to make a picture graph with a key of ☺ = 3 students.

Favorite Pet

Kind of Pet	Number of Students
Goldfish	12
Bird	15

1. How many ☺ will Kim draw for Goldfish?

Ⓐ 2　Ⓑ 3　● 4　Ⓓ 5

2. How many ☺ will Kim draw for Birds?

Ⓐ 2　Ⓑ 3　Ⓒ 4　Ⓓ 5

3. Jerel made a picture graph to show the number of sunny days his city had in June and July. This is the key to Jerel's picture graph.

Key: Each = 10 days.

How many sunny days do stand for?

Ⓐ 3　Ⓒ 30
Ⓑ 4　Ⓓ 35

4. Jamie saw 24 red cars and 16 blue cars. She made a picture graph to show her results. If △ = 4 cars, how many △s show the number of blue cars she saw?

Ⓐ 4　Ⓒ 8
Ⓑ 5　Ⓓ 16

5. Jeff took a survey about the snack his 26 classmates liked best. He used the data to begin making a picture graph. Complete Jeff's picture graph. Explain your work.

Favorite Snack

Crackers	☺ ☺ ☺ ☺
Fruit	☺ ☺ ☺

Key: Each ☺ = 4 students.

Possible answer: 16 students liked crackers. I subtracted 16 from 26 to find that 10 students liked fruit. I used the key and drew 2 ☺ and half of a ☺ in the fruit row.

Measurement and Data　　81

Lesson 82
CC.3.MD.3

Name _____

Use the graph for 1–3.

Carrie asked people at the mall to choose a favorite type of music. The bar graph shows the results.

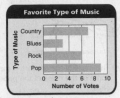

1. How many **more** people chose Rock than Blues?

Ⓐ 2　Ⓒ 4
Ⓑ 3　Ⓓ 9

2. How many people in all chose a type of music?

Ⓐ 4　Ⓒ 22
Ⓑ 16　Ⓓ 25

3. How many **more** people would have to choose Blues to have the same number of people choose Blues and Country?

Ⓐ 3　Ⓒ 6
Ⓑ 4　Ⓓ 7

4. Diego made a graph to show how many butterflies he saw in his yard each day. How many **fewer** butterflies did Diego see on Tuesday than on the day that he saw the most butterflies? Explain how you used the graph to find the answer.

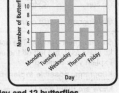

5 fewer; Sample explanation: the tallest bar, which is Wednesday, is the day he saw the most butterflies. The graph shows that he saw 7 butterflies on Tuesday and 12 butterflies on Wednesday. I subtracted 7 from 12 to find the answer.

82　　Measurement and Data

Lesson 83
CC.3.MD.3

Name _____

Use the table for 1–2.

Brendon wants to use a table with data about the number of oranges picked to make a bar graph.

Oranges Picked

Type of Orange	Bushels
Navel	15
Pineapple	12
Temple	10
Valencia	14

1. How many bars will Brendon have on his graph?

Ⓐ 2　　Ⓒ 9
● 4　　Ⓓ 16

2. Which type of orange will have the longest bar?

Ⓐ Navel
Ⓑ Pineapple
Ⓒ Temple
Ⓓ Valencia

3. Joey is making a bar graph to show how many pets his classmates have. Which pet will have the shortest bar in his graph?

Ⓐ 8 cats　　Ⓒ 4 dogs
Ⓑ 6 hamsters　● 3 horses

4. Martina is making a bar graph to show the 37 finches she saw in her garden from Monday through Friday. How tall should Martina make the bar to show how many finches she saw on Wednesday? Explain your answer and complete the graph.

Possible explanation: I added the finches she saw on Monday, Tuesday, Thursday, and Friday: 4 + 7 + 5 + 8 = 24. Then I subtracted 24 from 37, and drew the bar up to 13.

Measurement and Data　　83

Lesson 84
CC.3.MD.3

Name _____

Use the graph for 1–2.

A biologist made a bar graph to show how many samples of each type of marine life she saw on a dive.

1. Of which type of marine life did the marine biologist see the **fewest**?

Ⓐ Cow Fish　　Ⓒ Seahorse
Ⓑ Puffer Fish　Ⓓ Seaweed

2. How many more Cow Fish did the biologist see than Seahorses?

Ⓐ 1　Ⓑ 2　Ⓒ 3　Ⓓ 4

Use the graph for 3–4.

Nigel made a bar graph to show how many bushels of each type of orange are for sale at a fruit stand.

3. How many **more** bushels of Pineapple oranges and Navel oranges are there than Temple oranges and Valencia oranges?

Ⓐ 1 bushel
● 3 bushels
Ⓒ 7 bushels
Ⓓ 24 bushels

4. How would you use the graph to find out if there were more Navel and Pineapple oranges for sale or more Temple and Valencia oranges for sale?

Possible answer: I would use the data in the graph and add the total number of bushels of Navel and Pineapple oranges for sale and then the number of Temple and Valencia oranges for sale. By comparing the sums, I could tell which groups of oranges there were more of.

84　　Measurement and Data

Answer Key

Lesson 85
CC.3.MD.4

Use the line plot for 1–2.

Mr. Robinson's students made a line plot to show the number of hats they each have.

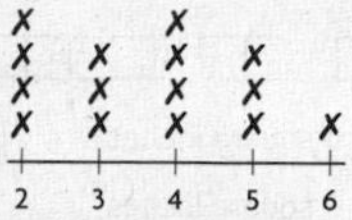

Number of Hats

1. How many students have 4 or fewer hats?

ⓐ 3   ⓒ 7

ⓑ 4   ● 11

2. How many students were included in the line plot?

ⓐ 13   ● 15

ⓑ 14   ⓓ 16

Use the line plot for 3–4.

Anna made a line plot to show the number of books each student in her class read for a reading contest.

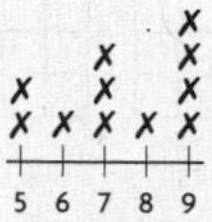

Number of Books Read

3. How many students read 9 books?

ⓐ 4   ⓒ 2

ⓑ 3   ⓓ 1

4. How many students read **fewer** than 8 books?

ⓐ 4   ● 6

ⓑ 5   ⓓ 7

5. Lewis made a line plot to show the number of hours students in his class spend at practice each week. Find the total number of students and the total number of hours. Explain how you found your answers.

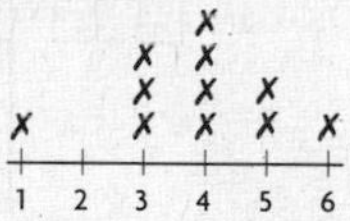

Number of Hours

Possible explanation: I found the total number of students, 11, by adding the number of Xs on the line plot. I found the total number of hours, 42, by multiplying each hour number by the number of Xs above it and then adding all the products together.

Measurement and Data   85

Lesson 86
CC.3.MD.4

1. Mrs. Williams uses an inch ruler to measure a flower in a picture. How tall is the flower to the nearest fourth inch?

ⓐ 2 inches   ⓒ $2\frac{3}{4}$ inches

● $2\frac{1}{4}$ inches   ⓓ 3 inches

2. Hector uses an inch ruler to measure a screw. What is the length of the screw to the nearest half inch?

ⓐ $1\frac{1}{2}$ inches   ⓒ $2\frac{1}{2}$ inches

ⓑ 2 inches   ⓓ 3 inches

3. Julio uses an inch ruler to measure a pencil sharpener. What is the length of the pencil sharpener to the nearest fourth inch?

ⓐ $\frac{1}{4}$ inch   ⓒ 1 inch

ⓑ $\frac{3}{4}$ inch   ⓓ $1\frac{3}{4}$ inches

4. Jade says her hair clip is $2\frac{1}{4}$ inches long. Do you agree? Explain.

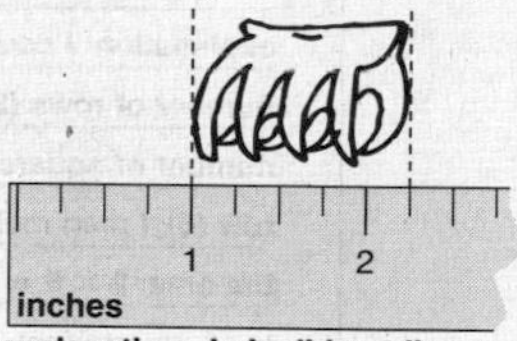

No; possible explanation: Jade did not line up the edge of the hair clip with the zero mark on the ruler, so the measurement is wrong.

86   Measurement and Data

Lesson 87
CC.3.MD.5,
CC.3.MD.5a

1. Greg drew the shape of the parking lot at school.

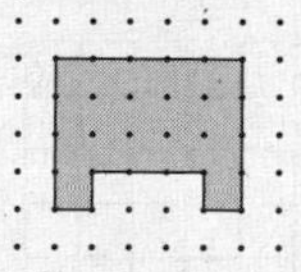

What is the area of the parking lot?

ⓐ 15 square units

● 17 square units

ⓒ 20 square units

ⓓ 22 square units

2. Mr. Chang wants to buy a rug for his living room. Which of the following does Mr. Chang need to find to know how much rug he will need?

ⓐ height of the living room

ⓑ length of the living room

ⓒ perimeter of the living room

● area of the living room

3. Sophia drew the shape of a path on dot paper.

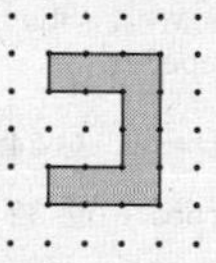

What is the area of the path Sophia drew?

● 8 square units

ⓑ 9 square units

ⓒ 10 square units

ⓓ 12 square units

4. Carmen needs to find the area for a project she is doing. Which could be Carmen's project?

ⓐ gluing string around a picture

ⓑ using wood to make a frame

● painting a wall

ⓓ putting a fence around a pool

5. The drawing shows the principal's office. Find the area of the principal's office and explain how you did it.

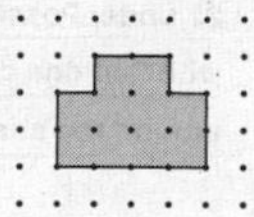

10 square units; Possible explanation: I counted the number of unit squares in the shape to find the area.

Measurement and Data   87

Lesson 88
CC.3.MD.5b,
CC.3.MD.6

Use the information for 1–3.

Billy is painting the background for the school play. The diagram shows the background. Each unit square is 1 square foot.

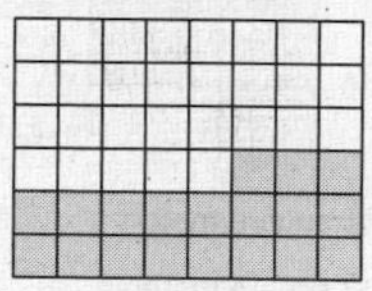

1. The shaded part shows the part Billy has already painted. What is the area of the background that Billy has already painted?

ⓐ 16 square feet

● 19 square feet

ⓒ 22 square feet

ⓓ 48 square feet

2. The white part shows the part Billy has left to paint. What is the area of the part Billy has left to paint?

ⓐ 19 square feet

ⓑ 21 square feet

● 29 square feet

ⓓ 32 square feet

3. What is the total area of the background that Billy is painting for the school play?

ⓐ 28 square feet

ⓑ 36 square feet

ⓒ 40 square feet

● 48 square feet

4. Naomi is putting square tiles on the floor of her bathroom. Each tile is 1 square foot. The diagram shows her bathroom. Find the area of the bathroom. Explain how you found the area.

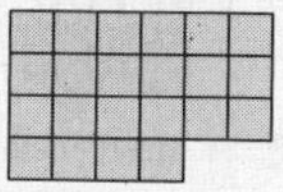

22 square feet; Possible explanation: each unit square is 1 square foot. I counted 22 unit squares in the diagram, so the area is 22 square feet.

88   Measurement and Data

Answer Key

1. The drawing shows Seth's plan for a footpath through his garden. Each unit square is 1 square foot. What is the area of Seth's footpath?

Ⓐ 14 square feet
Ⓑ 16 square feet
Ⓒ 18 square feet
Ⓓ 21 square feet

2. Keisha draws a sketch of a tile mosaic she wants to make on grid paper. Each unit square is 1 square inch. What is the area of Keisha's mosaic?

Ⓐ 9 square inches
Ⓑ 18 square inches
Ⓒ 20 square inches
Ⓓ 25 square inches

3. The drawing represents a vegetable garden in the Wilsons' backyard. Each unit square is 1 square meter. What is the area of the Wilsons' vegetable garden?

Ⓐ 7 square meters
Ⓑ 12 square meters
Ⓒ 14 square meters
Ⓓ 24 square meters

4. Roberto put square tiles down in the entryway. Each tile is 1 square foot. Write the area of the entryway floor. Explain how you found the area.

12 square feet; Possible explanation: I counted the number of rows (2) and the number of square tiles in each row (6). I then multiplied to find the area: 2 × 6 = 12, so the area is 12 square feet.

---

1. Brian drew these shapes. If the pattern continues, the next shape will have an area of 24 square units. What will be its length?

Ⓐ 4 units
Ⓑ 6 units
Ⓒ 8 units
Ⓓ 16 units

2. Brent uses carpet squares to make the pattern. Each unit square is 1 square foot. If the pattern continues, what will be the area of the fourth shape?

Ⓐ 27 square feet
Ⓑ 30 square feet
Ⓒ 42 square feet
Ⓓ 48 square feet

3. Julia uses tiles to make the pattern below. Each unit square is 1 square inch. If the pattern continues, what will be the area of the fourth shape?

Ⓐ 6 square inches
Ⓑ 8 square inches
Ⓒ 10 square inches
Ⓓ 12 square inches

4. Amy measured two rooms at her school. The first room is 8 feet wide and 10 feet long. The second room is 16 feet wide and 10 feet long. Describe how the lengths and widths of the rooms are related. Then use this information to explain how the areas of the two rooms are related.

Possible answer: the width of the second room is twice the width of the first room. The lengths of both rooms are the same. Because of this relationship between length and width, the area of the second room is twice the area of the first room.

---

1. Colby drew a diagram of his garden. Each unit square is 1 square foot. What is the area of Colby's garden?

Ⓐ 32 square feet
Ⓑ 30 square feet
Ⓒ 24 square feet
Ⓓ 20 square feet

2. The school office is shown. Each unit square is equal to 1 square meter. What is the total area of the school office?

Ⓐ 24 square meters
Ⓑ 30 square meters
Ⓒ 39 square meters
Ⓓ 48 square meters

3. Mrs. McCarthy's art studio is shown. Each unit square is equal to 1 square meter. What is the total area of Mrs. McCarthy's art studio?

Ⓐ 35 square meters
Ⓑ 27 square meters
Ⓒ 25 square meters
Ⓓ 21 square meters

4. Jake drew the diagram of his bedroom shown. Each unit square is equal to 1 square meter. Write the area of Jake's bedroom. Explain the steps you used to find the area.

13 square meters; Possible answer: I drew a horizontal line below the top row to divide the shape into two rectangles. I then multiplied to find the area of each rectangle and then added those areas to find the total area.

---

1. Irie draws a 4-sided shape on his paper that measures 8 inches on each side. What is the perimeter of the shape?

Ⓐ 8 inches   Ⓒ 24 inches
Ⓑ 16 inches   Ⓓ 32 inches

2. Yuko drew the shape of her garden on grid paper.

What is the perimeter of Yuko's garden?

Ⓐ 14 units   Ⓒ 16 units
Ⓑ 15 units   Ⓓ 17 units

3. Adam drew this shape on grid paper.

What is the perimeter of the shape?

Ⓐ 14 units   Ⓒ 10 units
Ⓑ 12 units   Ⓓ 9 units

4. A shape has 4 sides. Two sides measure 5 inches and two sides measure 8 inches. What is the perimeter of the shape?

Ⓐ 40 inches   Ⓒ 16 inches
Ⓑ 26 inches   Ⓓ 10 inches

5. Ling drew the shape of a hopscotch game on grid paper. Write the perimeter of the shape. Explain how you found the perimeter.

22 units; Possible answer: I started counting with 1 at one corner. I counted each unit around the shape.

Answer Key

1. Fiona bought a picture with a perimeter of 24 inches. Which picture did she buy?

Ⓐ 3 in. | 8 in. | 3 in.
8 in.

Ⓑ 4 in. | 6 in. | 4 in.
6 in.

Ⓒ 2 in. | 9 in. | 2 in.
9 in.

Ⓓ 7 in. | 5 in. | 7 in.
5 in.

2. Kim wants to put trim around a picture she drew. How many centimeters of trim does Kim need for the perimeter of the picture?

6 cm | 6 cm | 6 cm
6 cm

Ⓐ 6 centimeters

Ⓑ 12 centimeters

Ⓒ 24 centimeters

Ⓓ 36 centimeters

3. Mr. Gasper is putting wood trim around this window. How many feet of wood trim does Mr. Gasper need for the perimeter of the window?

2 ft
3 ft | 3 ft
2 ft

Ⓐ 6 feet   Ⓒ 12 feet

Ⓑ 10 feet   Ⓓ 13 feet

4. Dylan used a centimeter ruler to draw this square. Find the perimeter of Dylan's square and explain how you did it.

8 centimeters; Possible explanation: I used the ruler to measure the

length of each side of the square. Each side was 2 centimeters long. I then

added the lengths of the sides to find the perimeter: 2 + 2 + 2 + 2 = 8.

Measurement and Data   93

---

1. Natasha cut out a rectangle that has a perimeter of 34 centimeters. The width of the rectangle is 7 centimeters. What is the length of the rectangle?

Ⓐ 5 centimeters

Ⓑ 10 centimeters

Ⓒ 20 centimeters

Ⓓ 27 centimeters

2. Vanessa uses a ruler to draw a square. The perimeter of the square is 12 centimeters. What is the length of each side of the square?

s
s | | s
s

Ⓐ 3 centimeters

Ⓑ 4 centimeters

Ⓒ 6 centimeters

Ⓓ 48 centimeters

3. Mrs. Rios wants to put a wallpaper border around the room shown. She will use 36 feet of wallpaper border. What is the unknown side length?

10 ft
4 ft
7 ft | a
4 ft
3 ft

Ⓐ 6 feet   Ⓒ 14 feet

Ⓑ 8 feet   Ⓓ 28 feet

4. Frank uses 16 feet of fencing around the perimeter of a rectangular garden. The garden is 5 feet long. What is the width of the garden?

Ⓐ 11 feet

Ⓑ 6 feet

Ⓒ 3 feet

Ⓓ 2 feet

5. Mr. Rios has a rectangular rug. The perimeter of the rug is 28 feet. The width of the rug is 6 feet. Find the length of the rug. Explain the steps you used to find the missing length.

8 feet; Possible explanation: I drew a diagram, labeled each width 6,

and each length l. I knew the sum was 28, so 6 + 6 + l + l = 28,

I found the unknown number or length must be 8 feet.

94   Measurement and Data

Use the information for 1–3.

Sarah is building a garden in the backyard. She drew a diagram of one way to lay out the garden.

1. What is the perimeter of the garden?

Ⓐ 9 units

Ⓑ 12 units

Ⓒ 14 units

Ⓓ 18 units

2. What is the area of the garden?

Ⓐ 6 square units

Ⓑ 12 square units

Ⓒ 14 square units

Ⓓ 18 square units

3. Sarah wants her rectangular garden to have the greatest possible area, but she wants the same perimeter as shown in her diagram. Which could be the length and width of Sarah's garden?

Ⓐ 5 units by 4 units

Ⓑ 6 units by 3 units

Ⓒ 8 units by 1 unit

Ⓓ 5 units by 2 units

4. Kathy drew these rectangles on grid paper. Explain how the perimeters and areas of the rectangles are related.

Possible answer: both shapes have a

perimeter of 8 units. The area of the

square is 4 square units. That is greater

than the area of the shape on the left,

3 square units.

Measurement and Data   95

Use the information for 1–3.

Cheung drew two rectangles on grid paper.

A | B

1. What is the area of each rectangle?

Ⓐ A: Area = 6 square units; B: Area = 6 square units

Ⓑ A: Area = 6 square units; B: Area = 3 square units

Ⓒ A: Area = 14 square units; B: Area = 10 square units

Ⓓ A: Area = 7 square units; B: Area = 5 square units

2. What is the perimeter of rectangle B?

Ⓐ 5 units

Ⓑ 6 units

Ⓒ 8 units

Ⓓ 10 units

3. Which statement about the perimeters and areas of Cheung's rectangles is true?

Ⓐ The areas are the same and the perimeters are the same.

Ⓑ The areas are the same and the perimeters are different.

Ⓒ The areas are different and the perimeters are different.

Ⓓ The areas are different and the perimeters are the same.

4. Shawana used square tiles to make the rectangles shown. Compare and contrast the areas and perimeters of her two rectangles.

A
B

Possible answer: the perimeter of rectangle A is

16 units and the area is 12 square units. The

perimeter of rectangle B is 14 units and the area

is 12 square units. The perimeters of the two

rectangles are different, but the areas are the same.

96   Measurement and Data

Answer Key   **129**

Lesson 97
CC.3.G.1

Name _____

1. Abby drew a point. Which shows a point?

(A) •
(B) •———
(C) ———————
(D) ◄————►

2. Cyrus uses line segments to draw a shape.

How many line segments does Cyrus's shape have?

(A) 6   (C) 8
(B) 7   (D) 9

3. Four friends draw shapes. Rachel, Zoe, and Jorge draw closed shapes. Andy draws an open shape. Which is Andy's shape?

(A)   (C)
(B)   (D)

4. Jamey drew this shape.

•———————•

What shape did Jamey draw?

(A) line
(B) line segment
(C) point
(D) ray

5. Randy drew these two shapes. Classify each shape as *open* or *closed,* and explain how you know.

Possible answer: the shape on the left is closed because it starts and ends at the same point. The shape on the right is open because it does not start and end at the same point.

Geometry   97

Lesson 98
CC.3.G.1

Name _____

1. How many right angles does this shape appear to have?

(A) 0   (C) 2
(B) 1   (D) 5

2. Look at the shape.

Which **best** describes the marked angle?

(A) less than a right angle
(B) greater than a right angle
(C) a right angle
(D) a straight angle

3. Which describes the angles of this triangle?

(A) 1 greater than a right angle; 2 less than a right angle
(B) 1 greater than a right angle; 2 right angles
(C) 2 greater than a right angle; 1 less than a right angle
(D) 1 greater than a right angle; 1 right angle; 1 less than a right angle

4. Which capital letter appears to have an angle that is less than a right angle?

(A) H   (C) T
(B) L   (D) Z

5. Mrs. Simpson drew this shape. Explain how to classify the marked angle.

Possible explanation: I compared the marked angle to the corner of a sheet of paper. The marked angle is greater than the corner, so it is greater than a right angle.

98

Geometry

Lesson 99
CC.3.G.1

Name _____

1. Which shape is **not** a polygon?

(A)   (C)
(B)   (D)

2. Vance drew a polygon with 6 sides. What is the name of the polygon he drew?

(A) triangle
(B) pentagon
(C) hexagon
(D) decagon

3. A builder is using tiles on a bathroom floor. Each tile has 8 angles. What type of polygon are the tiles?

(A) decagon   (C) octagon
(B) hexagon   (D) quadrilateral

4. Kendall drew one closed shape using 5 line segments. Which shape did Kendall draw?

(A) quadrilateral
(B) pentagon
(C) hexagon
(D) octagon

5. Alex drew these four shapes. Circle the shape that is **not** a polygon. Explain why the shape you circled is not a polygon.

Possible answer: the circled shape is not a polygon because it is an open shape. All polygons are closed shapes made of line segments.

Geometry   99

Lesson 100
CC.3.G.1

Name _____

1. How many pairs of parallel sides does this hexagon appear to have?

(A) 0   (C) 3
(B) 1   (D) 6

2. Brad drew a quadrilateral. Which sides of the quadrilateral appear to be parallel?

(A) a and b   (C) b and d
(B) a and c   (D) c and d

3. Which word can be used to describe the dashed sides of the triangle?

(A) parallel   (C) point
(B) perpendicular   (D) quadrilateral

4. Sami uses straws to model a triangle. Which word can be used to describe the two dashed sides of the triangle?

(A) intersecting   (C) perpendicular
(B) parallel   (D) right

5. Brenton and Katie made a model of a polygon. Brenton said the two dashed sides shown are parallel. Katie said they are intersecting. Who is correct? Explain.

Brenton; Possible explanation: the dashed sides will never cross or meet each other, which is the definition of parallel line segments. Intersecting line segments will cross or meet somewhere.

100

Geometry

Answer Key

1. Hillary drew this shape.

Which word **best** describes the shape Hillary drew?

Ⓐ square   Ⓒ rhombus

Ⓑ rectangle   Ⓓ **trapezoid**

2. Cooper used toothpicks to make a shape.

Which **best** describes the shape Cooper made?

Ⓐ decagon   Ⓒ **square**

Ⓑ open shape   Ⓓ trapezoid

3. Edward says he drew a quadrilateral. Which of these could **not** be Edward's shape?

Ⓐ   Ⓒ

Ⓑ   Ⓓ

4. Helen drew this shape.

Which word **best** describes the shape Helen drew?

Ⓐ **rectangle**   Ⓒ square

Ⓑ rhombus   Ⓓ trapezoid

5. Aidan draws a shape with 4 sides of equal length and no right angles. Classify Aidan's shape using one or more of the following terms: *quadrilateral, rhombus, square, rectangle, trapezoid*. Explain how you classified the shape.

quadrilateral and rhombus; Possible answer: because the shape has 4 sides, it is a quadrilateral. Because the sides are of equal length, it is a rhombus. The shape cannot be a square or rectangle because it has no right angles.

Geometry   101

---

1. Melody draws a quadrilateral with 2 pairs of opposite sides that are parallel. Which could be the quadrilateral Melody draws?

Ⓐ   Ⓒ

Ⓑ   Ⓓ

2. Gina drew a quadrilateral that has 4 sides of equal length and 4 right angles. Which shape did she draw?

Ⓐ pentagon   Ⓒ trapezoid

Ⓑ **square**   Ⓓ triangle

3. Hannah drew a quadrilateral with exactly 1 pair of opposite sides that are parallel. Which shows a shape Hannah could have drawn?

Ⓐ   Ⓒ

Ⓑ   Ⓓ

4. Henry drew a quadrilateral that has 2 pairs of sides of equal length and 4 right angles. Which shape did he draw?

Ⓐ hexagon   Ⓒ trapezoid

Ⓑ pentagon   Ⓓ **rectangle**

5. Josie drew a quadrilateral with exactly 1 pair of parallel sides. Draw and classify a quadrilateral that could be like Josie's. Explain why you drew what you drew. **Possible drawing shown:**

trapezoid; Possible explanation: I drew a trapezoid because it has only 1 pair of opposite sides that are parallel.

102   Geometry

---

1. Which triangle appears to have 1 right angle and 0 sides of equal length?

Ⓐ   Ⓒ

Ⓑ   Ⓓ

2. How are triangles *L, M,* and *N* alike?

Ⓐ They all have 1 angle greater than a right angle.

Ⓑ They all have 1 right angle.

Ⓒ They all have 3 angles less than a right angle.

Ⓓ All of their sides are of equal length.

3. Ping drew a triangle that has 3 angles smaller than a right angle and 3 sides of equal length. Which shows Ping's triangle?

Ⓐ   Ⓒ

Ⓑ   Ⓓ

4. Brian drew a triangle that has 1 angle larger than a right angle and 0 sides of equal length. Which shows Brian's triangle?

Ⓐ   Ⓒ

Ⓑ   **Ⓓ**

5. Caden made triangles *A, B,* and *C.* Compare the angles and side lengths of Caden's triangles.

Possible answer: triangles *A, B,* and *C* all have 1 right angle and 2 angles less than a right angle. Triangles *A* and *C* appear to have 0 sides of equal length. Triangle *B* appears to have 2 sides of equal length.

Geometry   103

Use the Venn diagram for 1–3.

Polygons with
Right Angles   A

2. Patrick found some more shapes to sort. Which shape should he place into the overlap section of the Venn diagram?

Ⓐ   Ⓒ

Ⓑ   Ⓓ

1. Patrick used the Venn diagram to sort shapes. Which label could he use for part A?

Ⓐ Open Shapes

Ⓑ Quadrilaterals

Ⓒ Shapes with Sides of Equal Length

Ⓓ Shapes with 1 Right Angle

3. Patrick has the shape shown below. Where should he place the shape in the diagram?

Ⓐ part A

Ⓑ Polygons with Right Angles

Ⓒ overlap section

Ⓓ outside the Venn diagram

4. Kendra used a Venn diagram to sort shapes. Write a label she could use for circle A. Explain your reasoning.

Quadrilaterals   A

Possible answer: Polygons with Perpendicular Sides; I looked at the five shapes in circle A, including the shapes in the overlap section. All of the shapes had at least 1 pair of perpendicular sides, while the other three shapes did not.

104   Geometry

Answer Key

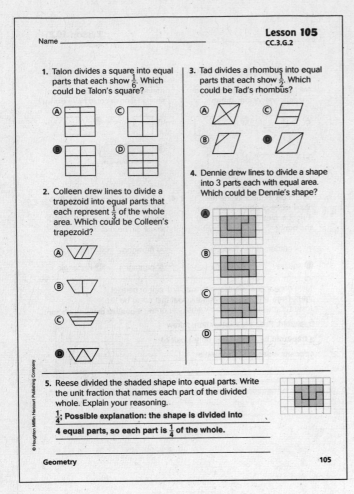

Name _____

1. Talon divides a square into equal parts that each show $\frac{1}{6}$. Which could be Talon's square?

   Ⓐ Ⓒ

   Ⓑ Ⓓ

2. Colleen drew lines to divide a trapezoid into equal parts that each represent $\frac{1}{3}$ of the whole area. Which could be Colleen's trapezoid?

   Ⓐ
   Ⓑ
   Ⓒ
   Ⓓ

3. Tad divides a rhombus into equal parts that each show $\frac{1}{2}$. Which could be Tad's rhombus?

   Ⓐ Ⓒ

   Ⓑ Ⓓ

4. Dennie drew lines to divide a shape into 3 parts each with equal area. Which could be Dennie's shape?

   Ⓐ
   Ⓑ
   Ⓒ
   Ⓓ

5. Reese divided the shaded shape into equal parts. Write the unit fraction that names each part of the divided whole. Explain your reasoning.

   $\frac{1}{4}$; **Possible explanation: the shape is divided into 4 equal parts, so each part is $\frac{1}{4}$ of the whole.**

Answer Key